NORTH LINCOLNSHIRE

Edited by Simon Harwin

First published in Great Britain in 2000 by
YOUNG WRITERS
Remus House,
Coltsfoot Drive,
Peterborough, PE2 9JX
Telephone (01733) 890066

HB ISBN 0 75432 204 1
SB ISBN 0 75432 205 X

FOREWORD

This year, the Young Writers' Up, Up & Away competition proudly presents a showcase of the best poetic talent from over 70,000 up-and-coming writers nationwide.

Successful in continuing our aim of promoting writing and creativity in children, our regional anthologies give a vivid insight into the thoughts, emotions and experiences of today's younger generation, displaying their inventive writing in its originality.

The thought, effort, imagination and hard work put into each poem impressed us all and again the task of editing proved challenging due to the quality of entries received, but was nevertheless enjoyable. We hope you are as pleased as we are with the final selection and that you continue to enjoy *Up, Up & Away North Lincolnshire* for many years to come.

CONTENTS

Althorpe and Keadby Primary School
    Louise Precious   1
    Jamie Guy   1
    Craig Jollands   1
    Kimberly Shields   2
    Ruth Smith   2
    Rachel Lee   3
    Sara Watson   3
    Catherine Nutt   4
    Sammi Carlile   4
    Christie Robinson   5
    Rebecca Quainton   5
    Chelsea Dawson   6
    Kayleigh Maxwell   6
    Thomas Knowles   7
    Zoe Robinson   7
    Lizzie Appleton   8
    Maxine Stringwell   9
    Lorna Marshall   9
    David Pepper   10
    Simon Cloherty   10
    Matthew Coulthard   10

Berkeley Junior School
    Inderpal Kaur & Chantelle Marshall-Rush   11
    Elizabeth Salmon   12
    Rebecca Johnson   12
    Katy Taylor   12
    Kimberley Warrillow   13
    Laura Greco   13
    Emma Blanchard   14
    Gavin Charlton   14

Castledyke Primary School
    Poppy McNaught   15
    Rachel Parker   15

Faye Scowen	16
Sam Milner	16
Sean Meffen	17
Alexandra Bawn	17
Jessica Henson	18
Cathy Seddon	18
Ashley Simpson	19
Leonie Pearson	20
Rachael Dunderdale	20
Jodie Sweeney	21
Lauren Johnson	21
Rebecca Vessey	22
Kirsty Walkington	22
Rosie Robinson	23
Gemma Carter	24
Christopher Lockham	24
Ryan Oldridge	25
Hayley Winstanley	25
Joe Brown	26
Josh Graham	26
David Skinner	27
Isabel Goodley	27
Kassie Pearson	28
Matthew Gregg	28
Paul Gregg	29
Alan Wharton	29
Shaunna Abdy	30
Ben Timmis	30

Grasby All Saints Primary School

Nikki Birkett	31
Laura Henson	31
Ben Wray	31
Darren Nigel Wells	32
Amy Peach	32
Alice Harriet Turland	33
Leah Robinson-Steer	33
Lucy V Melbourne	33

Rosie Cotterill 34
Claire Emily Andrew 35
Ross Oldershaw 36
Nadine Lawrence 36
Charlotte Eve Curtis 36
Joe Saunders 37

Henderson Avenue Primary School
Daniel Adderley 37
Stacey Ashcroft 38
Andrew Naylor 38
David Ray 39
Christopher Steed 39
Sarah Mitchell 40
Daniel Southern 40
Jodie Dickinson 41
Jamie Rayner 41
Melissa Papworth 42
Matthew Bishop 42
Natalie Watson 43
Scott Collins 43
Kirstie Atkinson 44
Katie Day 44
Natalie Shaw 45

Immingham St Andrew's Junior CE School
Abigail Seymour 45
Emma Blyth 46
Stephanie Griffin 46
David Haagensen 46
Kayleigh Snow 47
Luke Potterton 47
David Burnett 48
Stacie Robbins 48
Kye Southwell 49
Rachele Buckley 49
Laura Dixon 50
Bryony Cowley 50

Hannah Hart	51
Natasha Doy	51
Konrad Dyer	52
Gordon Burns	52
Adam Ladlow	53

Lincoln Gardens Junior School

Shaun Seaton	54
Hannah Birkby	54
Ben Blanchard	55
Cameron Stevenson	55
Hollie Coult	55
Jamie Vause	56
Lucy Foster	56
Thomas Davis	57
Laura Wilmot	57
Emma Holtby	57
Emily Kirkpatrick	58
Laura Crane	58
Amanda Fordham	59
Nicola Barnard	59
Christyarnna Berkeley	60
Catherine Shipley	60
Matthew Fleming	61
Blaine Blair Coomes	61
Natalie Sawford	62
Paul Weston	62
Joseph Rabbitt	63
Thomas Jordan	64
Lyndsey Potter	64
Rachel Clark	65
Gemma Langton	66
Mark Fowler	66
Leonie Walker	67
Joshua Mahon	68
Chloe Marsh	69
Amber Ross	69
Ian Whyatt	70

James Fletcher	70
Craig McLellan	71
Katie Cryer	72
Sam Crawley	73
Lois Ferraby	74
James Smith	75
Jodie Deas	75
Philip Drewry	76
Thomas Brasier	76
Mark Richards	77
Sadie Jackson	77
Beckie Hopkins	78
Jade Elston	78
Michael Vickers	79
Kimberley Turner	79
Laura Cook	80
Emma Picksley	80
Neal Rabbitt	81
Adam Sanderson	81
Amy Natasha Whitworth	82
Amy Hornsey	82
Nathan Wayne Fletcher	83
Hermione Cartwright	83
Louisa Vanessa Coombs	84
Vanessa Justice	84
Ashley McWhirter	85
Rebecca Escritt	85
Holly-Anne Rawson	85
Thomas Carnaby	86
Ashley Godson	86
Gemma Rawlinson	86

Normanby-By-Spital Primary School

Laura Cooke	87
Christopher Williamson	88
Rebekah Mayo	89
Holly Darby	90
Katie Louise Bavin	90

Samantha Reilly	91
Nichola Bratley	92
Nathan Cook	92
Amy Chandler	93
Emma Cook	93

Rochdale Road Junior School

Kayleigh Crook	94
Amy Downing	95
Jason Goodall	96
Georgina French	96
Rebecca Bradley	97
Sarah Store	97
Evette Brown	98
Tarnya Donald	98
Laura Skipworth	99
Jonathan Wren	99
Gemma Place	100
Paris Willey	100
Heidi Botfield	101
Elizabeth Snell	101
Craig Ryder	102
Leanne Brown	102
Danielle Brady	103
Francesca Bradley	103
Leanne Sloane	104

St Bernadette's RC School, Scunthorpe

Christopher Reed	104
Adele Robinson	105
Lucy Coulbeck	106
Darius Zhabhi	106
Amy Gravel	107
Natasha Trantali	107
Naomi Powell	108
Katie Trocko	108
Shaun A Mawdsley	109
Shaun McDermott	109

Melissa Lo 110
Adam Brady Birkett 110
Emma Blyth 110
Katie Blackburn 111
Annabel Igoe 111

St Michaels Primary School, Louth
Dominic Cummings 111
Anni Blades 112
Holly Brown 112
Melissa Atkinson 113
James Borman 113
Gemma Allison 114
Harvey Stott 114
Charlotte Simpson 115
Luke Pocklington 115
Anne Hickson 116
Matthew Evison 117
Abbie McRae 117
James Hicks 118
Rachel Dixon 118
Leon Murray 119
Chloe Hainesborough 119
James Leach 120
Katy Van Kempen 120
Christopher Lovely 121
Darren Espin 121
Thomas Richardson 122
Megan Tero 122
Emma Hardy 123

St Peter's CE Primary School, Cleethorpes
Jamie Freshwater 123
Joanna Barnard 124
Ryan Spence 124
Amy Waterman 125
Christopher Mortlock 125
Lacey Burke 126

David Curtis   126
Chloe Chambers   127
Nick Parker   127
Lianne Coultas   127
Chelsea Waterman   128
Hafsa Begum   128
Claire Sleight   129
Matthew Brown   129
Jonah Simmons   130
Sarah Stewart   130
Alex Crampton   131
Gemma Sargent   131
James Harrowing   131
Yasmin Spence   132
Jade Snowdon   132
Jessica Edwards   133
Jenna Young   133
Eleanor Johnson   134
Adam Brown   134
Gemma Kelly   135
Betsy Fairweather   135
Laura Smith   136

Saltfleetby School

Adam Beasley   137
Charmaine Gibson   137
Jodie Stephenson   138
Martha Rees   138
Jason Hill   139
Abigail Geeson   140
Christopher Beasley   140
Hayleigh Lee   141
Charlotte Kaye   141
Laura Bishell   142
Sophie Vines   142
Adam Mountain   143
John Mawson   143
Joanne Snelling   144

Wayne Bourne 144
Kerry Martin 145

Scamblesby CE School
Emily Duncumb 145
Emma Benge 146
Juliet Phillips 147
Andrew Lucas 148
Jack Noon 149
Rory Hannam 150
Robyn Hopper 151
Harriet Hopper 152
George Merrett 152
Katie Lucas 153
Elliot Towl 154
Emma Whitfield 155
Ian Askew 155
Eloise Middleton 156
Jonjo Hanson 157
Hannah Priestley 158
Martin Lovesey 159
Toby Hughes 160
Jessica Noon 160
Eleanor Middleton 161
Mark Epton 161
Matthew Whitfield 162
Adam Askew 162
Emma Shaw 163
Joseph Sears 163
Ciaran Melens 164

Scotter Primary School
Rebecca Downie 164

Western Primary School
Kirstie Howarth 165
Laura Wheatley 165
Matthew Donner 166

Adam Waterman   166
Christopher Turner   167
Louise Blood   167
Melissa Freeman   168
Rebecca Smalley   168

Yarborough Primary School
                    Lizanne Patrick   168
                    Hollie Meller   169
                    Richard Sharp   170
                    Catherine Wilson   170
                    Katie Harris   171
                    Lucy O'Nions   172
                    Sarah Baines   172
                    Matthew Doyley   173

The Poems

BUTTERCUP DAY

In my hand, I hold
A buttercup of gold,
A brave and shining fellow
In his coat of yellow.
With his golden eye
He stares into the sky,
And nods his rounded head
Wherever children tread.

Louise Precious (9)
Althorpe and Keadby Primary School

THE MOON IS . . .

Yellow and sparkling up in the sky
Sometimes crescent and sometimes full.
The moon is like a Milky Way.
It is in the middle of the sky
And shines upon the side of you.
When I look up at the sky
It is bright and also gloomy.

Jamie Guy (9)
Althorpe and Keadby Primary School

THE MOON IS . . .

The moon is shining blazing upon us.
The moon changes all in different shapes.
The moon is surrounded by millions of little stars.
The moon with its silver light catches everything.

Craig Jollands (9)
Althorpe and Keadby Primary School

THE MAGIC BOX

I will put in the box . . .

The tooth, of a growling Siberian Tiger,
the first teardrop that fell from my eye,
the cool winter breeze that brings snowflakes.

I will put in the box . . .

A roar of thunder, the lightning that crashed my mum's computer,
A pearl from the silent, underwater world,
A tiny puff of cloud from Mount Olympus,
   where the ancient gods lived.

I will put in the box . . .

A feather of a golden eagle, that hovers over her nest
And a whip of the whirly candyfloss from the circus.

Kimberly Shields (10)
Althorpe and Keadby Primary School

THE MOON

The moon is:

Brightly shining in the sky, like the sun
Changing colours, from grey to white, or white to silver.
Gleaming brightly on things on the ground
Stars all around the moon, singing in the dark, black sky.
The moon changing shape from full moon to half moon to crescent
moon.
Shining brightly on the trees, turning them to silver.

Ruth Smith (10)
Althorpe and Keadby Primary School

WORST THINGS

I can't stand cold wellies,
Or my mother's wobbly jellies.

My worst fruit is pears,
I can't stand the polar bears.

I can't stand chips and beans,
Or my sisters, the terrible teens.

I hate winters and all the nasty wind,
And my best shoes being binned.

Rachel Lee (10)
Althorpe and Keadby Primary School

MATHEMATICS

Mathematics is so good
Addition and subtraction and sums to learn
Easy sums on Tuesday
Mental maths is so hard
Always subtraction every day
At the moment trying to learn my addition
Concentrating people trying to work
Struggling people trying to get a merit.

Sara Watson (10)
Althorpe and Keadby Primary School

MY HOUND

My hound is a very strange hound,
because he never makes a sound.

He gets cosy near the fire,
and jumps in and out of wires.

First he eats his Pedigree Chum,
but I must say he's rather dumb.

When I say I'm going to the park,
he always starts to loudly bark.

When I try to sit down,
he seems to make a frown.

He does get muddy,
but he's still my best buddy.

Catherine Nutt (9)
Althorpe and Keadby Primary School

THE MOON

The moon is
Dazzling in the sky,
Changing size, full dull to crescent,
The moon is like a shiny bottle of fresh milk
Shining, changing things from dull to silver,
At night it stands out when I look up,
When I look up at the moon it reminds me of a silver ball,
Showing me the way around, when dark outside,
Shining, gleaming up above our heads.

Sammi Carlile (9)
Althorpe and Keadby Primary School

MY FISH

My fish whirls round and round
Like a merry-go-round.
His scales are like the golden sun glistening,
First he was a baby fish
But now he is four years old,
That is very old.
When I give him his food he sucks on my finger.
He is very greedy, he gulps all of his food down.
My fish has a very funny name,
He is called Fish Wish.
His fins are smooth and silky.

Christie Robinson (9)
Althorpe and Keadby Primary School

MISS ROBINSON

Miss Robinson is tall and pretty,
She's very smart, cool and witty,
She always gets us into trouble,
Especially the boys, gosh, they're in a puzzle.
She's got a very flashy car,
But it doesn't get her very far.
In my SATs I got a high score,
It made me jump up off the floor!

Rebecca Quainton (9)
Althorpe and Keadby Primary School

THE DINNER HALL

D   ropping food
I   n the dinner hall,
N   oisy pupils,
N   attering children,
E   ating chicken drummers,
R   inging knives and forks.

H   ot beefburgers and chips,
A   ngry dinner ladies,
L   unch being munched,
L   eftovers in the basin.

Chelsea Dawson (9)
Althorpe and Keadby Primary School

MY BONNIE RABBIT

My bonnie rabbit has stomping feet,
and she eats juicy meat.
She sleeps and sleeps all day long
and when she wakes up, she dances to a song.
Big floppy ears like candyfloss
and when she gets back, she eats the moss.
When she gets back with her big fat belly,
She sniff's something smelly.

Kayleigh Maxwell (10)
Althorpe and Keadby Primary School

WHAT THE TEACHERS DO AT HOME

When the teachers go home,
They sit on the sofa,
Watch the TV,
And balance chocs on their knees.

The teachers have a meeting
About horrid children cheating,
Then they go to bed and start sleeping,
And dream about the next day
When they get their pay.

And what did the teachers find at the schools?
Loads of children acting like fools!

So, all I can say,
On another school day,

It's going to be a bad day for teachers,
And a great day for cheaters!

Thomas Knowles (9)
Althorpe and Keadby Primary School

I WILL PUT IN THE BOX . . .

The last powerful ride on my horse's back.
The first time I giggled at my mum.
My first photograph took in the newspaper.
My last hug from my special grandad.
An old ornament I've had since I was born.
My first rattle that I held.
A feather from a brightly coloured parrot.

Zoe Robinson (10)
Althorpe and Keadby Primary School

SCHOOL

Time is ticking,
Naughty boys flicking,
Pencils around the room,
Bang bang boom.

Out to play,
Playing Simon Says,
Little ones falling,
Teachers calling.

Back inside,
Children tried,
To do work very good,
Like they always should.

Here comes PE,
They were doing animal acts like a bee,
Flutters around up and down,
As mad as a silly clown.

Getting changed,
'Christopher Grange,
Please stop talking,'
Shouted the teacher gawking.

'You can all go home,
And write a poem,
You can go to the shop,
So off you pop.

Lizzie Appleton (9)
Althorpe and Keadby Primary School

THE MAGIC BOX

I will put in the box . . .
A sharp pinch from an enormous crab,
A fang from a crocodile's dangerous jaw,
A mane from the roaring king of the jungle.

I will put in the box . . .
The last step from my great, great grandmother,
The first tooth that fell out of my mouth,
The smell of a scrumptious mulberry pie.

I will put in the box . . .
The last golden leaf to fall in autumn,
The first hair to grow on a baby's head,
The last sea shell to drift out to sea.

Maxine Stringwell (9)
Althorpe and Keadby Primary School

THE CAT

Pat the cat has got three legs,
She was born like that.
Her fur is like a rainbow in the sky,
A cuddly cat nice and warm,
She purrs like the humming of a bee all day long.
A creepy, crawly walk she's got,
She does it all the time,
She likes Felix cat food the best.

Lorna Marshall (9)
Althorpe and Keadby Primary School

THE MOON

The moon is . . .
Sparkling with the stars glistening all night,
The moon looks like a block of cheese,
Well that's what I thought when I was young,
Sometimes the moon looks like a banana,
Sometimes the moon looks like a ball,
Sometimes you can't even see the moon
Because it is so cloudy.

David Pepper (10)
Althorpe and Keadby Primary School

THE WONDROUS HAMSTER

A white patch hamster that's mainly brown,
He likes his bed and he's very adventurous,
Fur like a cat and a tiny pink tail,
His front feeding paws are like forks,
He monkey swings across the black steel cage,
He eats like a chipmunk chewing a nut.

Simon Cloherty (10)
Althorpe and Keadby Primary School

THE MOON

The moon is as bright as a glowing candle
In a dark room.
It shines over the Earth
And it sometimes looks like a block of cheese.
The sun shines on the moon and makes it glow
Like a light reflecting on a mirror.

Matthew Coultard (9)
Althorpe and Keadby Primary School

TEACHER'S CUP OF TEA

Mrs Bayley asked
Mr Callaway, and
Mr Callaway asked
Miss Fry
'Could we have some biscuits
For the teacher's cup of tea?'
Miss Fry asked
The shopkeeper
The shopkeeper
said 'Certainly
I'll go and tell
baker,
Now,
Before she goes to bed'

Miss Fry
She nodded
And went and told
The shopkeeper
'Don't forget the biscuit for
The teacher's cup of tea'
The shopkeeper
said sleepily
'You'd better tell
Mrs Bayley.'

Inderpal Kaur & Chantelle Marshall-Rush (10)
Berkeley Junior School

A POEM ABOUT A CHURCH

C hurchyards covered with beautiful flowers
H owling of the bells in the church
U pon the building the gargoyles haunt
R ight at the top of the church the battlements stand
C hristians sing in their holy voices
H igh churches stand for hours waiting for a new day to arrive.

Elizabeth Salmon (10)
Berkeley Junior School

VALENTINE'S DAY

Flowers, candy and hearts galore
Sweet words of love for those you adore
On this day comes love that's true
On Valentine's Day and all year through!

Rebecca Johnson (9)
Berkeley Junior School

APPLES

Juicy sensation
In a bright green slippery coat
The juice slurped slowly.

Katy Taylor (11)
Berkeley Junior School

THE EARTH

The Earth is a big round ball,
From outer space aliens call.

The Earth is a place for flowers to grow,
The stars in the dark sky glow.

The Earth is a place for people to live,
At Christmas presents they like to give.

The Earth has water and a big sea,
At the seaside children play with me.

On the Earth we have some roads,
On each side of the road are people's abodes.

On the Earth are stepping stones,
If you fall you will break your bones.

Kimberley Warrillow (10)
Berkeley Junior School

PURPLE

An evil colour which has been
Brought upon this world,
A guilty mind of the past,
A cruel spirit which goes on into the future,
A colour no one can understand,
A shadow of the night
Shooting down on us
Like a cloak of murders.

Laura Greco (10)
Berkeley Junior School

GOBLINS

There are goblins in my bathroom
And when laying in my bath,
They climb out of the plughole
With a great big *splash!*
They steal my soap and flannel,
Then they tickle my toes
And sometimes they pop all the bubbles
And they try to get up my nose.
My mum thinks I'm telling stories
But I certainly am not.
They disappear down the plughole
When I signal with a cough.
I am the only one who can see them,
They're magic you see,
So don't bother to come for a bath to my house,
You'll not see any goblins, only *me!*

Emma Blanchard (10)
Berkeley Junior School

BROWN

It is a dark, shaded place that no one can see into
And the sadness of imitating sounds disappearing into thin dust
A sobbing sound of echoing cries
And a dedicated scream inside your head
It is an Aztec leader who rules the land
It's the crack in an open door with the elderly world outside
It is the boredom of a child and the evilness of anger,
An ancient sign of speaking.

Gavin Charlton (11)
Berkeley Junior School

ON THE STAGE

Once more she stepped into the stage
And turned bright red with burning rage,
She really couldn't take much more
So what she did was faint to the floor.
The teacher said 'What is the matter?'
Her teeth really began to chatter.
The teacher stood and gasped and gulped
And with all this she turned to pulp.
Her arms and legs had gone like jelly,
She turned and looked at the actor Shelley.
The curtains closed
He legs turned blue.
She said 'I think I have the flu.'
She felt a stirring in her tummy,
She screamed 'Oh, I want my mummy.'

Poppy McNaught (10)
Castledyke Primary School

SWEET LITTLE HAMSTER

Deep inside the metal bars
Dwelt the cheeky smile of the small sweet hamster.
With deep red eyes that glare into mine
And a small pink tail bobs up and down.
Fur like velvet,
Claws like silver tinted blades
Shimmering in the sunlight.
Turning in his wheel like a spinning firework,
After a hard night's work eating,
Drinking and playing,
Tip-toeing quietly into his warm cosy bed.

Rachel Parker (10)
Castledyke Primary School

PRINCESS OF THE OCEAN!

Enchanted harmony.
She dances through her kingdom,
So free, so graceful,
Speaking to her loyal friends,
Whistling and clicking, so peaceful!

Her inquisitive eyes sparkle through the glistening ocean,
Her warm heart pounds with joy and happiness,
As she leaps in and out of the blue water,
Splishing and splashing, forbidding it to rest again!

She glides across the water, so silent, so silent,
Skimming through foam, like a soaring eagle,
Like a jewel in the crown,
She's the princess of the ocean!

Faye Scowen (11)
Castledyke Primary School

PERFECT WORLD

P   retty flowers
E   veryone quiet
R   ich hearted humans
F   riendly animals
E   xciting surprises
C   areful people
T   hankful mankind.

Obedient, polite and caring world.

Sam Milner (8)
Castledyke Primary School

SIR ALEX'S DREAM

Once more Sir Alex stepped into the ground
To complete his lifetime dream
To watch his team shout and scream
Man U went out, played the best
And made Sir Alex really proud
When the team scored a goal
There was a big cheer from the crowd
Beckham ran down the line
He crossed the ball ever so fine
Yorkey hit it with his head
And left the keeper lying dead
Cole skipped by two defenders
Crossed it to Giggs
And everyone shouted headers
Jaap Stam made a brilliant tackle
So everyone started to battle
Scholes hit the back of the net
And everyone started to bet
The game was over
And Man U won with brilliant style.

Sean Meffen (11)
Castledyke Primary School

INSIDE MY HEAD

Inside my head I think about coming to school to meet all my friends.
Inside my head I think about my mum, dad and my sisters.
Inside my head I think about what's going on outside.
Inside my head I think about everything because it's all just a dream.
Inside my head I think about what the next day's going to be like.

Alexandra Bawn (8)
Castledyke Primary School

ENGLAND

Onto the hallowed turf they stepped,
This would be their last time,
Wembley Stadium was being sold,
Certainly for more than a dime.
The England squad looked glum and sad,
Would the result be good or bad?

The ref blew his whistle for the start of the match,
Straight away David Seaman made an excellent catch,
The second half started at nil-nil,
The England players went in for the kill.

Gary Neville passed to Philip,
Who passed to Alan Shearer
Who was nearer,
To Cole,
Who scored the winning
Goal!

Jessica Henson (10)
Castledyke Primary School

MY DOG REBEL

A gentle giant, black and tan,
No greater friend to any man,
Head on one side, he'll listen to me,
With looks of love and serenity.

A playful companion, a trustworthy guard,
His temperament changes from docile to hard,
If I were in danger he'd take care of me,
In the home he'd prevent a burglary.

He doesn't need much, just love, food and fun,
A cosy warm bed and me and my mum,
I'll love him forever right to the end,
He'll always be my special friend.

Cathy Seddon (10)
Castledyke Primary School

ONCE MORE HE STEPPED ONTO THE PITCH

Once more he stepped onto the pitch
Hoping not to have a hitch,
The whistle blew
And of they flew
(The rain was teaming
But the crowd was still screaming)
He was using his skills
Which would pay his bills
He was dribbling
His legs were quivering
He scored a goal or two
While the crowd went whoo!

He was thrashing them
While crashing into them
At the same time as fowling them
The goals were going in both left and right
The game became tight!
The crowd was loud
The players were proud
As the final whistle blew
The score was eighteen-two!

Ashley Simpson (9)
Castledyke Primary School

MOTHER AND CUB

Once more she stepped into her lair,
And growled and shook her mangy hair.

She glared lovingly at her cub,
Who stared back, searching for grub.

A warm breeze weaved in and out of them,
When the sun was setting outside again.

She coiled herself around her son,
As the birds outside raised a soft hum.

Slowly, quietly, they fell asleep
And as they slept, there was not a peep.

Leonie Pearson (11)
Castledyke Primary School

DOLPHIN

Gliding through the water,
Flying through the air,
Catching a breath as it flies,
Through the air like a flying fish or even a bird.
Its large toothy grin and its large dorsal fin flapping,
Signs of a very happy mammal.
It gently creeps up on its prey,
Gently eats it anyway.
Plays all day and never stops,
Swims all day, day after day.
In front of ships, under large waves,
The dainty, delicate dolphin gives delightful and delusive sights.

Rachael Dunderdale (11)
Castledyke Primary School

THE HAUNTED HOUSE

At the haunted house the gates are swaying
Go inside and the walls are shaking
Feel the carpets moving and waking
The lamp is turning and casting spells
While the table is shaking its mystical bells
Near the table hear the windows groaning
From the outside hear the door moaning
The chairs are running and playing catch
While the sofas are having a football match!
The TV is poking a little pig
While the curtains are trying on a wig!
If you're going there count me *out*
I can tell you that without a *doubt!*

Jodie Sweeney (9)
Castledyke Primary School

THE HAUNTED HOUSE

Once more he stepped into the 'Haunted House'
With great courage he said 'Who is here?;
He shouted it again mainly out of fear
(Such loud howling noise hung around)
He tripped and heard a mysterious sound,
He turned around, and became very scared.

The ghost looked down and just glared,
Floating and shimmering, then a shivering,
He leapt down in big leaps,
He wanted to give him a little treat.

Instead he lead him to a river,
And then began to disappear.

Lauren Johnson (10)
Castledyke Primary School

WHEN I AM OLDER

When I am older
I will be a doctor to help the unwell.
I will be a cleaner to polish and clean up.

When I am older
I will be a nurse to help the worst.
I will be an actor to do plays for children.

When I am older
I will be a teacher to teach children.
I will be a dancer to be in a pantomime.

When I am older
I will have a diary that says
Keep out!

Rebecca Vessey (7)
Castledyke Primary School

WHEN I AM OLDER

When I am older
Shops will be buzzing
Hair will be fuzzing
Shoes will be walking
People will be talking
Mothers will be battered
Hair will be plaited
Computers will be whirling
Hair will be curling.

Kirsty Walkington (8)
Castledyke Primary School

GAMES LESSONS

Feet kicking
Children scoring
Teacher sighing
Whistle blowing

Sticks banging
Legs moving
Teacher shouting
Game ending

Children queuing
Ball flying
Teacher crying
Bats whacking

Stumps swaying
Bail falling
Teacher gasping
Keeper catching

Ball bouncing
Rackets hitting
Teacher groaning
Partner losing

Scrum heaving
Legs freezing
Teacher moaning
Bodies hurting.

Rosie Robinson (8)
Castledyke Primary School

MY PERFECT WORLD

My perfect world
Would have chocolate
To have lots and lots of chocolate and sweets
Collect flowers from fields
To have a pet dog
To have six friends
To have twenty pounds
To help people
Grow fruit and vegetables
To have a holiday in Disneyland
For there to be no bullies
To stay at school forever
For there to be peace on Earth forever and forever.

Gemma Carter (8)
Castledyke Primary School

MY PERFECT WORLD

To get sweets
To collect roses
To go 'Boo!'
And go to the zoo
To have my own bedroom
And go abroad to Africa
Try do my shoelaces
And go to school late
I'd love to have a warthog
Or even a pet dog
To have a drink from the bar
Or even be a film star!

Christopher Lockham (8)
Castledyke Primary School

WHEN I WAS YOUNG

When I was one
I couldn't do a thing
When I was two
I said my first word
When I was three
I could walk
When I was four
I could talk
When I was five
I put my hand in a beehive
When I was six
I fell in some pits
When I was seven
My uncle went to Heaven
When I turned eight
I really liked cake.

Ryan Oldridge (8)
Castledyke Primary School

MY PERFECT WORLD

The ground made of chocolate
The flowers smell so nice you can smell them all day
And the trees are standing
Up so tall and are so green they look perfect
The rivers made out of melted toffee
Now this is my perfect world
It's always hot and families are with you all the time
Nobody falls out with anyone.
                    Absolutely perfect.

Hayley Winstanley (9)
Castledyke Primary School

INSIDE MY HEAD

Inside my head I'm always thinking,
Inside my head my eyes are blinking;
Inside my head my brain cells are growing,
Inside my head I'm thinking of going.

Inside my head I'll make world peace,
Inside my head I'll give everyone cold a fleece;
Inside my head I'll give you what you need,
Inside my head I'll stop the greed.

Inside my head I'm gonna go, go, go,
Inside my head I'll grow, grow, grow;
Inside my head I'll stop a war,
Inside my head food will be stored.

Inside my head you'll have some food,
Inside my head you'll never be rude;
Inside my head you'll have some books,
Inside my head you'll have some food from your cooks.

Joe Brown (8)
Castledyke Primary School

IN MY HEAD

In my head
It's time for bed
For goodness sake
I'm wide awake
Here I am in my pyjamas
Wishing I was in the Bahamas
I really have to go to sleep
And dream of me driving a Jeep.

Josh Graham (8)
Castledyke Primary School

When I Am Older

When I am older
    I will be
A teacher with
    A French
Moustache with
    Gold specs,
With a top hat,
    A grey suit,
And light blue
    Eyes,
Shiny hair,
    Smooth black skin,
A friendly smile.

David Skinner (9)
Castledyke Primary School

The Tiny Mouse

Once more he stepped into his house
Looked in the mirror and saw he was a mouse
He just could not believe his eyes
And told the people it was all lies
Could anybody sort out this mystery?
'Cause now he's turned into a bumblebee
Let's hope some people enter in
Or we're gonna have to throw him in the rubbish bin
Come and pop in, check it out
And when you come in please don't shout
If you do then we've had it
We're going under the sea for a bit.

Isabel Goodley (10)
Castledyke Junior School

MY PERFECT WORLD

Everything made out of Cadbury's chocolate.
No sisters
'Cause they're all big blisters.
No school,
'Cause all of the teachers are fools
Except a few . . .

Your parents never tell you off.
You never have to think
And when you want something you just blink.
It is always hot
And everyone drinks juice from an apricot.
You are never freezing or cold
And you never grow old.

Kassie Pearson (9)
Castledyke Primary School

WHEN I AM OLDER

When I am older I want to be
A very strong wrestler, no one can thrash me.

When I am older I want to be
A strong swimmer, that's me.

When I am older I want to be
A champion football player, that's me.

When I am older I want to be
A great school teacher, that's what I want to be.

Matthew Gregg (9)
Castledyke Primary School

WHEN I'M OLDER

When I'm older I'll be a boss .
And boss you about
Okay?

Or shall I be a racer?
And run very fast.

No I'll be a model
And impress you with my style!

I know I'll be a super hero
And beat up all the baddies

Yes I'll be a super hero!
And fly away . . .
Home!

Paul Gregg (9)
Castledyke Primary School

SHARKY

Shark, silent killer
Swims gracefully through the water,
Body streamlined but rough,

Teeth as razors,
Tears the flesh of its prey like a piece of paper,
It attacks, the prey had no chance.

Food devoured,
Hunger crushed,
The shark swims off slowly,
Into the darkness.

Alan Wharton (10)
Castledyke Primary School

INSIDE MY HEAD

Inside my head
Everything's made of chocolate
It's just my imagination.

Inside my head
I think something's dead
Is it my imagination or what?

Inside my head
I'm thinking, I'm thinking very hard
But nothing's happening.

Inside my head
Sometimes I get lost
But find myself again.

Inside my head
There are a lot of things going on
Like being a champion of swimming.

Shaunna Abdy (8)
Castledyke Primary School

INSIDE MY HEAD

Inside my head there's my brain
Inside my head I have a conscience to tell me
Whether I should do something or not
Inside my head I have an image in my mind
- I think I'm in chocolate land!
Inside my head you must think I'm mad
Because you think I'm from the zoo.

Ben Timmis (9)
Castledyke Primary School

WHAT IS A CAR?

A car is a roaring monster,
A purring kitten at the traffic light,
A wide load on a lorry,
As heavy as my mum.
It's as white as a cloud,
As shiny as a hammer,
As fast as a puma.

Nikki Birkett (11)
Grasby All Saints Primary School

SWIMMING

Swimming is great fun
When you come out you are dripping wet
It keeps you fit
Mates in the swimming pool always splash each other
It is for big ones and little ones
No one should miss out on swimming
Going swimming is good for you.

Laura Henson (10)
Grasby All Saints Primary School

THE JUNGLE

The jungle is a giant lime
The centre is the stones and canopies
The green is a splodge of green paint on blue paper
The liveliness is a disco party
The sun is a bright light on a dismal day
The sun's ray is the heat of a fire-breathing dragon.

Ben Wray (11)
Grasby All Saints Primary School

WHAT IS A ... CAR?

A car is a roaring monster
As it pulls when it spins,
When it's flat out it goes like a rocket,
With big fat allies
That sparkle in the sun,
The colour is red that's highly polished,
With seats that fit you like a glove,
And a steering wheel made of leather,
With bumpers and spoilers
And lowered as well,
With a boom box for added sound,
And a tail pipe too,
A car is a dream.

Darren Nigel Wells (10)
Grasby All Saints Primary School

THE AEROPLANE

The propeller goes round and round
As the aeroplane zooms off the ground.
Soon it is as high
As a bird in the sky.
Houses and people are little dots
Just like Jelly Tots.
On top of the world, in mid air
You can see a foal and mare.
My friend and me
Look down on all we see.
You can hear a noisy sound
Coming down upon the ground.

Amy Peach (9)
Grasby All Saints Primary School

MY PET GHOST

My cool pet,
Is stranger than most,
The weirdest you've ever met,
'Cause it's a pet ghost!

But the strangest thing about my pet,
Is not a scar or mark,
Yet the scariest ghost you've ever met,
Is terrified of the dark!

Alice Harriet Turland (11)
Grasby All Saints Primary School

MY HAMSTER INKY

My pet hamster is named Inky
She is very small and dinky.
She's always in her bowl eating all night long
But in the daytime you go to take a peek and she's gone.
But today she's in her wheel whizzing away
She was sleeping all of yesterday.

Leah Robinson-Steer (11)
Grasby All Saints Primary School

THE PENCIL POT

The pencil pot is a planet of its own,
A planet of snow, with fireworks coming out of the centre
The table on which the pencil pot sits is the universe
In which the planet rests at night.

Lucy V Melbourne (11)
Grasby All Saints Primary School

My Job

I've had a great day
I'm feeling fine,
I got my monthly pay
For the first time.

My job's a social worker
And work from seven till three,
So if you need some home help
You know where I will be.

I mostly work in the office
But I sometimes go outside,
My old job was a chiropodist
But the smell nearly made me die.

I hope to be an actress
And work with Hollywood stars,
I'd like to be like Ursula Andress
And drive in fast sports cars.

I'd hate to be a writer
It takes me ages to write a book,
I'd rather be a fighter
Even better . . . be a cook.

If I was a cook I would cook apple pie
I would be mad on decoration,
And would not be shy.

I think I will stick at the job I have now
I am better at that, ·
I'd write a book but don't know how
It would make me look a prat.

A social worker suits me
Now I've got to go,
So goodbye, au revoir, and even tally ho.

Rosie Cotterill (11)
Grasby All Saints Primary School

KATE AND HER DOG, JACK

There once lived a girl called Kate,
Who had a dog called Jack,
Wherever she went she was late,
And every time, her mum gave her a smack.

One day a terrible thing happened to her dog,
It was most truly unexpected,
Suddenly Jack turned into a frog,
'Oh dear,' cried Kate, as to her mum she fled.

This time her mum was not cross,
In fact to stop her crying,
She gave her some candyfloss,
At once she stopped and started flying.

Around the room she flew,
Knocking down pictures as she went,
Her mum was in such a stew,
Shouting, 'There'll be an accident!'

Claire Emily Andrew (9)
Grasby All Saints Primary School

THE SPACESHIP

Here it comes the UFO,
The doors opening oh no.
Look at the green blob,
it looks like a frog.
It's coming to grab us,
We better back up,
Here it comes . . . dash!
It's a lazer gun better run!

Ross Oldershaw (10)
Grasby All Saints Primary School

WHAT IS THE SUN?

The sun is a gold milk top kicked high in the sky.
It is a ball of dragon's fire!
It is a handprint dipped in yellow paint.
It is a yellow beachball kicked in the sky.
It is a golden coin fallen down from Heaven!

Nadine Lawrence (11)
Grasby All Saints Primary School

WHAT IS . . . THE RAIN?

The rain is a shower of diamonds,
Falling from black velvet pillows.
It is sparkling crystals in the sun.
It is pins tapping on the glass window.
It is brown spots of paint on a concrete path.

Charlotte Eve Curtis (9)
Grasby All Saints Primary School

WHAT IS . . . A CLOUD?

A cloud is a big soft ball floating in the sky,
It's a comfy lump of candyfloss that caught my eye.
They race to the finish as quickly as they can,
When they're tired they block out the sun.
They put on their raincoats when it's about to rain,
When they're happy they scatter snowflakes so people can play.
When they fight they send out bolts of lightning,
And when the wind is happy it sends out a breeze
And when they are angry they send out a tornado or hurricane.
The clouds splash rain when they cry.

Joe Saunders (9)
Grasby All Saints Primary School

BUILT IN THE GRAVEYARD

The house is in the graveyard
It stands on top of the hill
The graves are falling over and nobody cares
All around the bare trees shiver in the cold wind,
Sad and lonely the flowers lie abandoned
No longer do people gather around the graves
By the newly dug grave a lone mourner stands
Through his mind the questions are repeating
Why now? Why you? Why me?
I am alone in the dark, come back please
Come back I need you to help me with the kids.
I won't be able to look after them all.

Daniel Adderley (9)
Henderson Avenue Primary School

Signs Of Danger

Next to the cemetery, stands the abandoned house.
Through the basement window we see shadows.
Across the mist our feet are guided nearer, nearer, nearer.

Before us we hear chanting
Around our feet the mist is creeping
Into the house the mysterious shadows lead us.
Throughout the house we see flickering lights.

Onwards the candles flicker,
Suddenly the lights go out and
We are left in total silence,
In the dark.

Stacey Ashcroft (10)
Henderson Avenue Primary School

The Haunted House

In front I see a silent house
Built on a silent hill.
It has been abandoned for many years
I walk slowly to the house
The shutters are banging against the windows
I see a light, the door slowly opens
Spirits fly into the air
Then I walk slowly to the door
The candle falls into the air.

Andrew Naylor (9)
Henderson Avenue Primary School

THE GHOUL'S GREENHOUSE

Behind the old abandoned church,
There lies a greenhouse, a ghoul's greenhouse.
Through the window we see a wave of death,
Dead plants hanging out of their pots.
Spirits rise from the wrecks,
Swirling spirits, swirling spirits scream a deafening chorus.

Indian ghouls rise chanting a cold, chilling song,
Our eyes start falling, the plants start calling
'Stay, stay away!'
We run to the church,
We get tied up by mad, maniac flowers.

The spirits of the long dead float, float into our bodies,
We go cold, very cold,
We freeze right on the spot,
We rise and float off,
Leaving our bodies behind.

David Ray (9)
Henderson Avenue Primary School

THE HAUNTED HOUSE

Through the mist on a cold and gloomy night
I saw a house standing empty and alone.
Through the windows I could see dark, moving figures
I could hear ghostly noises.
The spirits are guiding me towards the door
It opens, I am led by something up the stairs
I feel someone touch my back'
Without looking back I make my escape.

Christopher Steed (9)
Henderson Avenue Primary School

THE FORBIDDEN GROUND

Onwards we are led into the forbidden ground.
There is not a noise, not a sound.
Beyond the gate there lies a mist all around.
In front of us a ramshackled house stands
Something is drawing us in
Maybe an invisible hand.
Behind the graveyard, is the place where the house rests
We have never seen it before.
Why can we see it today?
Will it be here forever?
Will it choose to stay?
Many a person has gone inside
But they never come out again
Will we choose to go in or not?

Sarah Mitchell (9)
Henderson Avenue Primary School

THE ABANDONED HOUSE

Through the grey, swirling mist we see a house, an abandoned house.
The broken, ragged shutters are swinging, creaking eerily.
We're drawn to the door, slowly it opens.
We see remains of old candles in the flickering lights.
On the landing a dark figure moves.

We're guided up the stairs by something or someone.
Above us the sound of ghostly wailing - then silence.
After that they never make another noise.

Daniel Southern (9)
Henderson Avenue Primary School

THE FORGOTTEN HOUSE

Through the dank, grey mist
We hear wolves howling and trees rustling.
Behind a high, haunted hill
Stands an abandoned house.
Beneath us the floor creaks
And the door slams shut.
Through the grimy windows
We see evil spirits swirling
Around the tall hill
In the dark, mysterious wood.
The dusty clock strikes twelve
Then there is silence, silence.

Jodie Dickinson (10)
Henderson Avenue Primary School

THE CHURCH

Through the stained glass windows I look
The wind is pulling me closer, closer.
In front of me the door flies open
Beyond I hear a whistling noise.
The door slams shut
Then the light shines through the windows
As the sun sets, the spirits of the dead swirl around in the mist.

Jamie Rayner (9)
Henderson Avenue Primary School

THE HAUNTED HOUSE

Through the ghostly garden,
We see an abandoned house.
We knock on the door,
The door creaks open
Onwards we walk.

All around us there are cobwebs and dust
In front there stands a grandfather clock
Under our feet the floorboards creak.

In front of us there is a door wide open
On the floor there lies a doll,
It's laid down as if frightened of something or someone
As we go to the door we hear a noise, a ghostly noise.

Melissa Papworth (10)
Henderson Avenue Primary School

THE ABANDONED CHURCH

Down the dark part of the street there is an abandoned church.
Windows are smashed, shutters hanging off their hinges.
The fences are broken and tiles are falling off the roof.
A man walks past and is drawn to the church by a noise.
He hears the screams from the long dead.
He sees candles from many, many years ago.
Then silence and darkness, complete darkness.

Matthew Bishop (10)
Henderson Avenue Primary School

THE HAUNTED HOUSE

Beyond the village, past the dark, mysterious woods
Stands a house, all alone and empty.
A long gone family lived there, but they disappeared.

No one knows where they went.
Their spirits are still in the haunted house.
As we enter, our feet are guided to another door.

It slowly opens
I see a shadow
Onwards we tiptoe
We hear a sound like a figure on the creaking floor
It gets louder
I hear a noise it's behind me .
I look, but there's no one there.

Natalie Watson (10)
Henderson Avenue Primary School

THE HAUNTED HOUSE .

Through the mist the spirits are coming.
The abandoned house stands lonely and still.
A shadow draws us to the dusty porch.
The door creaks open.
A figure moves around on the cobweb landing.
We go up the stairs, behind us the door slams shut.
We move on, we see a door slide open.
A swirling spirit is in the grounds of the haunted house.

Scott Collins (9)
Henderson Avenue Primary School

BUILT ON A FORGOTTEN GRAVEYARD

Beyond the trees a house is standing
Within an old forgotten graveyard.
Through the gloomy windows, shadows are floating everywhere
Drawing me closer to the abandoned house.
As I approach the house the mist is swirling all around my feet
As I walk through the door dusty cobwebs
Hang from the corners of the room.
In front of me are stairs, my feet are guided up them.
Before my eyes the door creaks open.
Onwards the mysterious figure leads me
Towards a painting of someone from long ago.
Up rise the spirits of the long dead.

Kirstie Atkinson (9)
Henderson Avenue Primary School

THE GHOSTLY CHURCH

Behind the dark and gloomy trees
There is a church, abandoned by all but the dead.
Out through the windows, float strange, mysterious noises.
The door creaks open, the noise grows louder.
Hesitant steps take us forward
Our eyes are met by darkness
Silence drifts around the room
Whoever or whatever was there - is not there now.

Katie Day (9)
Henderson Avenue Primary School

THE HAUNTED HOUSE

High on a hill stands a house
Behind are the ghostly trees
With hands that are waiting to grab you.
If you go to the house
The spirits come back from the dead
In the house they will be there.

Later the door will open slowly, it will creak
Is there anybody there? Nobody answered.
Then he left and the spirits went back to the dead.
When will they return?

Natalie Shaw (10)
Henderson Avenue Primary School

IF I COULD BE A . . .

If I could be an animal
I would be a bird
I would fly free in the breeze
Eat loads of delicious fish
Fly along, singing, 'Ke, ke, ke'
Calling all the birds to follow me.
My coat would be fancy, colourful and bright
So I could reflect my colour in the daylight sun.
If I was a bird
I would hunt at night
Catch my prey and say goodnight, 'Ke, ke, ke'
And I would be a friendly bird
If any one wanted to see me
'Ke, ke, ke, ke.'

Abigail Seymour (10)
Immingham St Andrew's Junior CE School

IF I COULD BE . . .

If I could be an animal
I would be a parrot
I'd eat dry food and peanuts
I'd look like a Furby.
I sound like a human
I move as fast as an aeroplane
I'm pretty friendly
I am very chatty.

Emma Blyth (9)
Immingham St Andrew's Junior CE School

IF I COULD BE . . .

If I could be an animal
I would be a rabbit.
I'd be black and fluffy
Bouncing around the garden
Eating carrots
I'd be friendly and gentle
Always twitching my nose.

Stephanie Griffin (9)
Immingham St Andrew's Junior CE School

IF I COULD BE A . . .

If I could be an animal
I would be a monkey
I'd eat coconuts
I'd lay around and sleep
And remember I will always be loveable.

David Haagensen (9)
Immingham St Andrew's Junior CE School

IF I COULD BE A . . .

If I could be an animal
A bird I would be
I would peck worms from the ground
Like a woodpecker
Look very colourful and furry like a bear
Stroke me like a pet.
I would move slowly and
Spread my wings like a plane
Sing so beautifully all day long
Be so sweet and very kind
I would love to be a bird.

Kayleigh Snow (9)
Immingham St Andrew's Junior CE School

IF I COULD BE . . .

If I could be an animal
I would be a mouse
I would scuttle around the house
Eating cheese
Yum, yum
If another mouse tried nicking my cheese
I would stare at it with my blue eyes
Attack it with my sharp teeth squeaking.

Luke Potterton (9)
Immingham St Andrew's Junior CE School

IF I COULD BE A . . .

If I could be an animal
I would be a cat
Eating lovely Whiskas
Sleeping on a soft cushion
Being stroked at night
Miaowing for cat biscuits
And I love getting in the way
I would sleep on the end of a bed
Run for my scratch-post
Always go to the toilet outside
Never scratch the furniture
Except when my parents are out
When I'm out people would say
What a beautiful, black cat
And my name is *Cookie*.

David Burnett (10)
Immingham St Andrew's Junior CE School

IF I COULD BE A . . .

If I could be an animal
I would be a cat
Drinking out of my bowl
I would look at myself.
I'd have a cute face
I'd like to call my friend softly
I'd love to be a pussycat.

Stacie Robbins (9)
Immingham St Andrew's Junior CE School

SUN'S JUST OUT

Sun's out
Children about
Bells ringing
Clocks ticking
Boys running
Girls skipping
Bells ringing
Clock going
Men running
Mum calling
Just snoring.

Kye Southwell (9)
Immingham St Andrew's Junior CE School

IF I COULD BE A . . .

If I could be an animal
I would be a dolphin
I will swim swiftly from place to place
Eat the fish and greet the people
That come and play with me.
I will dive in the water
Eeek, eeek, eeek!
And show my shiny, silver skin.

Rachele Buckley (9)
Immingham St Andrew's Junior CE School

CHILLING OUT WITH FRIENDS

Hannah dancing
Laura prancing
Crystal creeping
Natasha sleeping
Ashley talking
Vicky walking
Kerry coughing
Cherie scoffing
Jade racing
Zarnia tracing
Jenna screaming
Rebecca beaming.

Laura Dixon (9)
Immingham St Andrew's Junior CE School

HANGING AROUND WITH FRIENDS

Hannah's playing
Rebecca's laying
Laura's talking
Sarah's walking
Laura's running
Victoria's humming
Amy's clapping
Crystal's tapping.

Bryony Cowley (8)
Immingham St Andrew's Junior CE School

IN THE PARK

In the park babies cry
Birds fly
Children singing
Church bells ringing
Boys fighting
Girls struck by lightning
Mums and dads sitting around
Trees are brown
Children nicking hats
Dogs chasing hats.

Hannah Hart (8)
Immingham St Andrew's Junior CE School

AT THE BEACH

Dads driving
We're arriving
Toddlers behaving
Mums sunbathing
Fish splashing
Seagulls passing
People screaming
Children sneezing
Friends leaving.

Natasha Doy (9)
Immingham St Andrew's Junior CE School

KOSOVO WAR

In Kosovo there is a tragedy
All Kosovo is covered in soldiers
Mums are starving, so their children can eat
Dads are getting killed and made slaves.
Houses - blown up
Solders - shooting people
People are escaping to England.
It's on the news
You are lucky to live here
If you live there
You risk
Death

Konrad Dyer (10)
Immingham St Andrew's Junior CE School

DOG

The dog is black
Short fur
It likes to run and play
With its tongue out.
It likes to chase sticks
It likes to chase balls
It likes to chase cats
It likes to chase me.

Gordon Burns (9)
Immingham St Andrew's Junior CE School

SUMMER

Here comes the sun boiling the land
Everyone sweated and were crawling
They crawled hand by hand.
The sun started to make them sweat
Most people started to get sun burns
Because they didn't put on any sun cream.
Everyone was closing their curtains
Trying to get to the ice cream
Everyone was looking for shade.
Searching far to fill their thirst
Everyone had a shelter which they made
To fulfil their shelter search
It's too late the heat's got to them.
Mirages were appearing everywhere
All the women, children and men
They were searching everywhere.
They were gasping for water
For death and for survival
Even the fountains have stopped watering
For a lot have got divided.
Everyone is a traveller for the thirst
Most people say there's a bad curse
Upon us so we must travel.

Adam Ladlow (9)
Immingham St Andrew's Junior CE School

I'M ARRESTED NOW

I robbed a bank yesterday
I might even rob today.
Oh no, there's a copper!
I will just shoot this shopper.
I had better quickly run
I haven't got time to get a bun
There's a bike
Next to a boy called Tike
I'll swipe it from a tray.
I'll go through the park and into town
I saw the policeman frown
Oh no, I've run into a policeman
Now I'm in jail because of that man
But I was let out early
And now I'm going to murder Shirley.

Shaun Seaton (9)
Lincoln Gardens Junior School

WINTER COMES

Winter comes
    with water frozen.
Winter comes
    with icicles on roofs.
Winter comes
    with Christmas coming.
Winter comes
    with Santa on his way.
Winter comes
    with lots of snow.

Hannah Birkby (8)
Lincoln Gardens Junior School

SUMMER

Summer comes with a big shine
Summer comes with sandals on feet
Summer comes with glasses on people
Summer comes with children playing
Summer comes with pools out
Summer comes with an ice cream van
Summer comes with boys playing football.

Ben Blanchard (8)
Lincoln Gardens Junior School

SUMMER

Summer comes with the sun shining
Summer comes with the birds whistling
Summer comes when the bees are here
Summer comes when we are warm
Summer comes when clouds are wide apart
We like summer.

Cameron Stevenson (8)
Lincoln Gardens Junior School

SUMMER COMES

Summer comes with yellow sunshine
Summer comes with happy holidays
Summer comes with people on the beach
Summer comes with big colourful sunglasses
. Summer comes with comfortable sandals.

Hollie Coult (9)
Lincoln Gardens Junior School

MY BIRTHDAY

My birthday comes with a large present
My birthday comes with a Happy Birthday!
My birthday comes with a good day out
My birthday comes with a good night out.
My birthday comes with a big balloon
My birthday comes with a round birthday cake.
My birthday comes with a piece of wrapping paper
My birthday comes with a large card.
My birthday comes with a long party
My birthday comes with a big bouncy castle
My birthday comes with a candle.

Jamie Vause (9)
Lincoln Gardens Junior School

SUMMER

Summer comes with a shining of the sun,
Summer comes with a cockerel screeching,
Summer comes with a holiday on the beach,
Summer comes with clear blue skies.
Summer comes with a bird that chirps every day,
Summer comes with a white cloud passing by,
Summer comes with a stinging of wasps,
Summer comes with the owl tu-whit tu-whooing at nights.
Summer comes with clear blue seas
Summer comes with a paddling pool out
Summer comes with the people talking.

Lucy Foster (8)
Lincoln Gardens Junior School

MY BROTHER

My brother comes with a crash of the cymbals,
My brother comes with lots of bumpy wrinkles,
My brother comes with a lot of loud noise,
My brother comes with some naughty boys.
My brother comes with lots of sobbing,
My brother comes with absolutely . . . nothing!

Thomas Davis (9)
Lincoln Gardens Junior School

MY BIRTHDAY

My birthday comes with a loud bang of balloons,
My birthday comes with a family - hands full of gifts.
My birthday comes with a lovely piece of cake,
My birthday comes with a day out to a restaurant.
My birthday comes with a fantastic sleep-over,
My birthday comes with a delicious tea party.

Laura Wilmot (9)
Lincoln Gardens Junior School.

CHRISTMAS DECORATIONS

The tinsel wiggled and jiggled as I tried to put it up.
The tree poked and prodded me as I turned around.
I fell over with a crash.
The baubles laughed as I fell to the ground.
I'm sure I heard the tree snigger!

Emma Holtby (10)
Lincoln Gardens Junior School

ANIMALS! ANIMALS! ANIMALS!

That elephant has a very loud stamp,
He's been in a river so he's damp.
This animal has a mighty roar,
He is a lion so he can keep the law!
This tiger has some stripes,
Although there are lots of types.
There he is swinging in a tree,
Over there is a chimpanzee.
I hear the birds all cawing,
I think I hear a bear snoring.
All the crocodiles are snapping,
While they are splashing they are rapping.
There are all the dolphins splashing deep,
That slope over there is not too steep.
There's an eagle nesting on the cliff,
The eggs are rock-hard and so stiff.

Emily Kirkpatrick (8)
Lincoln Gardens Junior School

ABOUT MY PETS, RAT, CAT AND BAT

I had a ginger cat,
Who held Pat the rat,
And jumped out of his hand,
And found a hairband.
Then ran in a hole,
And ended up in the North Pole.
Then Pat the rat,
Had a go at my ginger cat
And then my black bat,
Laid on a wide mat.

Laura Crane (8)
Lincoln Gardens Junior School

MY SUMMER POEM

Summer comes
    with a splash in the swimming pool.
Summer comes
    with a shout at the big park
Summer comes
    with a picnic basket yum, yum.
Summer comes
    with a sandy beach with ice-cream.
Summer comes
    with daylight at my bedtime.
Summer comes
    with racing on my dream bike.
Summer comes
    with a big cheeky smily face.

Amanda Fordham (8)
Lincoln Gardens Junior School

GOING OUT TO PLAY

Running out of class at play,
Children hoping to get away.
Teachers shouting all around,
Do not push him to the ground!
Someone tripped up and cried,
He went to hospital and nearly died.
'Don't worry!' said his teacher.
'Mum won't be mad she will just beat you.'
Later he went home to go to bed,
But just then he looked at his shed
And saw a big balloon at night,
With two old men having a fight.

Nicola Barnard (8)
Lincoln Gardens Junior School

MY BIRTHDAY

My birthday comes
  every year.
My birthday comes
  with friends.
My birthday comes
  with presents.
My birthday comes
  with happiness.
My birthday comes
  with joy.
My birthday comes
  it's the time for me to be happy.
My birthday comes
  with cousins to see.
My birthday comes
  I think about people on their birthday.

Christyarnna Berkeley (8)
Lincoln Gardens Junior School

THE HARE AND THE TORTOISE

The hare thought she could win the race,
That's why she said I could run to space.
The race started, the tortoise sighed,
Off we go, and plodded along at the side.
On the way she stopped to sign
Autographs, one, one, one at a time.
The hare stopped to have a nap
'Cos she thought the tortoise would need a map.
In the end the tortoise won,
The hare said, 'That wasn't fun.'

Catherine Shipley (10)
Lincoln Gardens Junior School

THE HARE AND THE TORTOISE

Rum-te-tum-te-tum
The hare is faster than the tortoise
Rum-te-tum-te-tum
They have a good race
Rum-te-tum-te-tum
The hare signs autographs in the run
And she eats green grass
Rum-te-tum-te-tum
At the end of the race
Rum-te-tum-te-tum
The tortoise has won
Rum-te-tum-te-tum
The hare is shocked and the fans call hare
Not fair!

Matthew Fleming (9)
Lincoln Gardens Junior School

THE HARE AND THE TORTOISE

The hare thinks he can beat the tortoise,
The hare is very fast,
They have a race,
Speedy's got pace.
Slocum's very slow.
The hare signs autographs,
Eats grass and sleeps the day away.
Slocum passes, wins the race
And the hare's devastated.
Lightning's now the tortoise's name,
And we can't say any more.

Blaine Blair Coomès (9)
Lincoln Gardens Junior School

My Dancing Hobby

I've been dancing all today,
In the middle of May.
Got exams all this week,
Let's all have a little peek.

I'm satisfied I've got this far,
Now I get a chocolate bar.
Last week I got some ballroom shoes,
My nanny has gone on a cruise.

Now I've got a competition,
And I've learned a new position.
Now I've got some jazz shoes,
Now my nanny's off her cruise.

Ann is my dancing teacher,
Louise drinks a whole beaker.
Louise makes an excellent team.

I like dancing every day
In the middle of May.

Natalie Sawford (10)
Lincoln Gardens Junior School

Riding On My Bike

I like riding on my bike,
Though it's not a modern bike.
I got it from the skip,
Although it was a tip.

It was yellow, black and blue,
And it was as sticky as glue.
It went as fast as a rocket,
It will not fit in my pocket.

I like riding on my bike,
Though it's not a modern bike.
It was yellow, black and blue,
And it was as sticky as glue.

Paul Weston (11)
Lincoln Gardens Junior School

BACK SEAT DRIVING

Driving down the M6,
Got stuck in a jam because of sticks.
They had fallen off a lorry,
Everybody said they were sorry.

Eventually we start moving,
Started again hooters tooting.
We came to a junction,
But we could not function.

The car broke down,
Dad had a frown.
He acted like a pig
And did a silly gig.

Dad got elected to be a ballroom host,
He pretended to be a ghost.
They chucked him out in a haste,
They just have not got taste.

He went on Top of the Pops
Then they took him to the cops.
He got put in a back stage jail,
Then he turned ever-so pale.

Joseph Rabbitt (11)
Lincoln Gardens Junior School

WINTER

Winter comes
    with frost biting at my toes.
Winter comes
    with snow settling on my fingers.
Winter comes
    with children throwing snowballs around.
Winter comes
    with everybody singing Christmas carols.
Winter comes
    with footprints in the snow.
Winter comes
    with animals hibernating in the ground.
Winter comes
    with children making snowmen.
Winter comes
    with cars sliding on the road.
Winter comes
    with icicles hanging from houses.

Thomas Jordan (8)
Lincoln Gardens Junior School

I LIKE DANCING

I like dancing and it's full of joy,
When I do my spins I'm like a toy.
Get it right and I'll get a chocolate bar,
Quite often it's a giant Mars bar.

I've got a private lesson at half-past eight,
I got there just a little bit late.
Tara said, 'That was great.'
And my friend said, 'I'm your mate.'

Soon it came to trophy time,
I hope one of those big ones is mine.
My mum said, 'I hope she's come first.'
'Yes,' Dad said, 'She's not the worst.'

Lyndsey Potter (10)
Lincoln Gardens Junior School

SUMMER

Summer comes
   with a bright shining sun.
Summer comes
   with long races won.
Summer comes
   with a blue clear sky.
Summer comes
   with white clouds passing by.
Summer comes
   with swimming in the sea.
Summer comes
   with busy buzzing bees.
Summer comes
   with children throwing balls.
Summer comes
   with people growing tall.
Summer comes
   with seagulls squawking.
Summer comes
   with adults walking.
Summer comes
   with school holidays.

Rachel Clark (8)
Lincoln Gardens Junior School

PLAYING ON MY PC

I've been playing on my PC,
Except when I'm having tea.
I bought a brand-new disk
I put it away because of the risk.

It was made in '99
It is called PC Time.
I played Solitaire
In my big comfy chair.

I bought a brand-new game,
My mum bought the same.
I was linked to the Net
My mum printed-out 'To Let'

I didn't know what it meant,
When I worked it out the phone line went.
We turned it off 'cos of the Millennium Bug
At twelve o'clock we gave a hug.

I like playing on my PC
Although it's not free.

Gemma Langton (11)
Lincoln Gardens Junior School

THE HARE AND THE TORTOISE

One day a hare sneered at the tortoise,
'If we raced you could cough in my dust.'
'You're on, I'll race you,' he said in a slow voice.
The hare sped off in a gust of dust.

The race started, Speedy Hare sped off.
He only stopped to sign autographs.
While Speedy slept Slocum crept off.
When he won the hare was eating a bun.

'Woohoo I win.'
'Do you want a bet?'
'Oh no I lost
You're lightning fast.'

Mark Fowler (9)
Lincoln Gardens Junior School

THE HARE AND THE TORTOISE

The hare thought she was the fastest around
but nevertheless is what she found.
She challenged the tortoise to a race,
'I'll beat you!' she said just in a pace.
In a bound and a leap I'll be home before tea.
I'll stop only once, only twice I'm so fast.
I could go round twice in a flash.
They set a date for the race at once
They started the race at their own special pace.
At four o'clock sharp they began their race.
Bang went the shotgun, zoom went the hare
But Slocumb the tortoise could only just stare.
The hare was ahead so the tortoise said
And having a nap round the bend.
Humming to himself he passed an elf
Who took no glee in seeing him.
Then suddenly he passed the finishing post
And was most surprised when he won.
The medal was red, gold, silver and blue.
They called the tortoise Speedy .
The hare finished later than sooner.
'Hip, hip hooray! I won! I won!'
'No you don't,' they all said.

Leonie Walker (9)
Lincoln Gardens Junior School

RIDING ON MY BICYCLE

I like riding on my bicycle,
With my best friend called Michael.
I got it from Rusty's
Off a man eating bread which was crusty.

I like riding on my bike,
It's better than having to go on a hike.
I just oiled by bike chain,
It took an hour, a total pain.

I've ridden up to Ashby Ville,
I've even ridden fast up Sunny Hill.
My tyre started to slump,
I had to got get it pumped.

I like riding on my bike,
Although it's not a motorbike.
I got it from a skip,
It was a disgusting tip.

I like riding on my bicycle,
It is so much fun to cycle.
It is fun to bike to the shop,
And then go home for some chops.

I like riding, it's a star,
I have been very far.
I love my bike it is great,
Finding it must have been fate.

Joshua Mahon (10)
Lincoln Gardens Junior School

THE HARE AND TORTOISE

The hare thinks she is the fastest
And said to the tortoise
'You are so slow, and I will give you a race.'
The hare ran off and the tortoise walked.
The hare took a nap
Then came tortoise, he went past.
The tortoise crossed the finish line
And won the race
And then came the hare
'I win I win I win'
'No the tortoise won''
After that everyone said
The tortoise is faster than the hare.

Chloe Marsh (10)
Lincoln Gardens Junior School

THE DOG AND HIS SHADOW

A dog one day had a piece of meat,
He had it tucked up in his mouth.
It was so big it was like an open sheet,
He kept turning and turning until he was south.
He saw a dog in the river,
His meat was much, much greater.
So the dog jumped and knew it was liver
He jumped as high as he could,
Then much much later . . .
He found out
It was his shadow in the river!

Amber Ross (10)
Lincoln Gardens Junior School

I LIKE RIDING ON MY BIKE.

I like riding on my bike.
It's better than doing a hike.
I bought it from a guy in town
When I left he gave a frown.

I rode it all the way home,
I ran over a potted gnome.
Even thought it is not mine,
I ride it in my spare time.

It was made in '99,
Now it's all mine, mine, mine.
Oil went all over the floor,
I act as if I'm poor.

My bicycle fell to bits.
I need some helpful tips.
I got it from a man on a hill,
He said he was from Brazil.

Ian Whyatt (11)
Lincoln Gardens Junior School

WWF'S DX

I love playing wrestling,
I hate it when the bell rings.
My favourite wrestler is X Pac
Compared to Kane he's a dot.

His finisher is the X Factor,
Knocks 'em down like a tractor.
He does Bronco Busters to Kane.
X Pac's got a big brain.

DX his team help him out,
Whenever he makes a shout.
X Pac v Kane today,
X Pac got choke-slammed straight away.

James Fletcher (10)
Lincoln Gardens Junior School

RIDING ON A BUS

I've been riding on a bus,
Even though it's not a rush.
I caught it when I was at the bus stop,
With a drink of cherryade pop.

It was made in '42,
In a factory near the loos.
I saw Horris on the door,
And he gave me a big chore.

I ride on it to go to school,
It always runs out of fuel.
But I never, ever care,
I don't think it's very fair.

It's very old but at least it's mine,
I mend it in my extra time.
Just last week I changed the fuel
But I still think it's very cool.

I like riding on my bus,
Even though people think it's a fuss.
I like riding on my bus,
Even though people think it's rush.

Craig McLellan (10)
Lincoln Gardens Junior School

WEMBLEY - SCUNTHORPE VS ORIENT

The date is 29th May
And on a journey we began
To those famous twin towers of Wembley
London here we come
Iron, iron, iron

Once there Wembley Way beckoned
As we walked those famous steps
Side by side with the Orient
Our fleet of fans tread
Iron, iron, iron

As Wilcox lead out our heroes
To cheers from our 15,000 fans
Not knowing where we were going
To be next season division two or three
Iron, iron, iron

With the game only six minutes old
Alex turned in delight
For his dream of scoring at Wembley
Had come true in the colours of yellow and blue
All the fans erupted
Was this going to be our day?
Could we hang on eighty-five minutes more
For the glory to come our way?
Iron, iron, iron.

As the clock struck 4.45
Our heroes were still 1-0 up
Then with the whistle to his lips
He blew our heroes into division two
The glory had come our way
And we will always remember that day
That day we went to Wembley
Iron, iron, iron.

Katie Cryer (10)
Lincoln Gardens Junior School

I LIKE RIDING ON MY BIKE

I've been riding on my bike,
Even though it's not a Nike.
I got it from the mall,
Even though the shop was small.

It was made in '93
In a factory in Torquay.
It said 'Y Frame' on the side,
Even though it had no guide.

It is young and it is mine,
I clean it in my spare time.
Just last week I took it to Stoke,
Because I broke a spoke.

I like riding on my bike,
Even though it's not a Nike.

Sam Crawley (10)
Lincoln Gardens Junior School

CHRISTMAS

Ten heavy snowmen standing in a line,
One lost weight, then there were nine.

Nine fat robins hopping on a gate
One suddenly burst, then there were eight.

Eight ugly angels flying up in Heaven,
One flew far away, then there were seven.

Seven little elves collecting little sticks,
One got squashed, then there were six.

Six of Santa's reindeer very much alive,
One fell through a cloud, then there were five.

Five mini fairies spying through a door,
One got caught, then there were four.

Four juicy turkeys hiding behind a tree,
One got cooked, then there were three.

Three poorly pixies all had the flu,
Unfortunately one died, then there were two.

Two naughty Santa thieves on the run,
One got caught, then there was one.

One huge Santa having lots of fun,
He got carried away, then there was none.

Lois Ferraby (11)
Lincoln Gardens Junior School

I LIKE PLAYING MY FOOTBALL

I've been playing with my brothers,
Though he doesn't bother.
Last night I played this game,
It always has a silly name.

Next day I played football,
Then I went to the mall.
The sunshine it is very hot,
It was like I was in a pot.

I did not like it,
So I just hit my sister's zit.
My sister just cried,
It was like I was fried.

I just read a book,
Then I just had a look.
At this word further more,
I just read a little more.

I like playing football,
And I like going to the mall.

James Smith (10)
Lincoln Gardens Junior School

THE SUN CRAWLED

The sun crawled up and peered along the horizon,
The clouds appeared from nowhere.
Together they pushed the moon away.
They're here for another twelve hours,
The start of another day.

Jodi Deas (10)
Lincoln Gardens Junior School

PLAYING COMPUTER GAMES

I like playing computer games,
It's a thing of many names.
I've got five of them myself,
I had to sell one off my shelf.

My mum she plays all night long,
It's even hard to write a song.
We've only just got the Internet,
So my sister lost the bet.

My sister always wants to play,
So I have to make her pay.
I just hope today's the day,
'Cos my mum has to pay.

I always dream of completing a game,
'Cos that is going to be my aim.

Philip Drewry (10)
Lincoln Gardens Junior School

JACK AND THE BEANSTALK

There was a boy who had a cow
He needed money but didn't know how
To market he went to sell
Everyone on the way he had to tell.

A man came walking the other way
What a handsome cow I say
I'll buy your cow for a bean
The biggest stalk was soon to be seen.

Thomas Brasier (9)
Lincoln Gardens Junior School

THE BOY WHO CRIED WOLF!

There was a boy who watched his sheep,
He always wanted a long long sleep,
One day he played a trick,
So he could go and pick
All the leaves off the trees
And visit Mr Kees,
So the boy cried wolf,
The people came in a gulf,
There was nothing there,
They ran their hands right through their hair,
Two days later,
The wolf did come,
And the boy was gone.

Mark Richards (10)
Lincoln Gardens Junior School

I CAN SEE . . .

Out of the window I can see
A tiny little bumblebee.
Two great big schools
And a man with tools.
A little girl, a little boy
Both playing expensive toys.
Running on the field is a shrew
You can't catch it, and it can't catch you!
'Dinnertime!' shouted Mum
So of I run to fill my tum.
I hope I live forever more
So I can tell people what I saw!

Sadie Jackson (8)
Lincoln Gardens Junior School

WOLF WOLF

There was a boy who looked after the sheep,
Late at night while the villagers were asleep,
When one night the boy was bored and cold,
He sat there and had an idea, so we're told,

He jumped up and shouted, oh so loud,
Screaming and yelling there's a wolf around,
The villagers got up and ran so fast,
Oh the naughty boy did laugh,
The villagers should have smacked him,
Or told him off but they thought him dim,

The next night when all was dark,
He did it again, oh what a lark.
But the following night a wolf was there,
Oh the little boy was very scared.
He screamed, he shouted, he jumped about,
But no one came, no one heard his shout,
So the wolf ate all the sheep
And the little boy, no don't weep.

Beckie Hopkins (9)
Lincoln Gardens Junior School

IN THE STREET

The cars moaned in the traffic, crawling along
As the postbox ate the letters.
The buildings stood there watching,
Grinning at the sight.
The lamppost jumped out,
As the yellow lines screamed, 'Go away!'

Jade Elston (11)
Lincoln Gardens Junior School

THE BOY WHO CRIED WOLF

There once was a boy who looked after sheep
Who dozed in the sun all day.
When he got bored he played a prank
And gave a loud cry of 'Wolf, wolf.'
All the farmers heard the boy
And came with guns and forks.
When they got to the field they found no wolf
Just a lazy boy grinning.
The farmers went angrily back to work
Next day the boy played the prank again
And gave a loud cry of 'Wolf'.
Again the farmers came with guns and forks.
Again they found no wolf and returned to work.
Later that day the wolf did come.
The boy cried 'Wolf' but nobody came to help.
Forever after, the boy never lied again.

Michael Vickers (10)
Lincoln Gardens Junior School

DEEP IN A DESERT

Deep in a desert a tiger lay,
Where an Indian man was walking one day.
The tiger lay waiting for prey,
Suddenly the man started to run away.
His teeth were sharp,
Loud was his roar,
The Indian ran ever more.

Kimberley Turner (8)
Lincoln Gardens Junior School

TREASURE TROVE

I saw a sea that was blue.
I saw a ship that had some crew,
I saw some divers they had a key,
They invited me under the sea.

There we saw a treasure chest,
So we unlocked it finding a fisherman's crest.
There was a cup that on it said Burt,
All the rest was covered in dirt.

The divers gave me a dirty look,
As if I had turned into a crook,
I put it back into the chest
And went up for air and had a rest.

Laura Cook (8)
Lincoln Gardens Junior School

DOWN IN THE SEA

Down in the water deep,
I creep.
Divers down in the sand,
What a brilliant land.
They meet a man,
And discuss a plan.

Down in the cool waters,
The man with his two daughters,
Float back up.
They found an old antique cup.
They got some water, do you want a drink?
Don't drop it, it might sink!

Emma Picksley (8)
Lincoln Gardens Junior School

ANIMALS

I saw a wild hog,
That turned into a fast dog.
I saw a slow cat,
That acted like a cute rat.
There was a shabby pony,
That was called friendly Tony.
I saw a shy whale,
That was very very pale.
There was a cold mouse,
In the tiny house.
There was a smelly cow,
And it didn't know how!
There was an invisible car
And it was made of thick tar
And a cool dish,
And it was full of hot fish.
There was a bossy fox,
That was packed tight in a box.

Neal Rabbitt (9)
Lincoln Gardens Junior School

THE COLOURFUL SEA

Deep in the sea where the barrier lay
A boy went diving at the beginning of the day
Massive clams open wide
Under sand colourful starfish hide
Rough crabs as red as blood,
And ever high the sea has a flood.

Adam Sanderson (9)
Lincoln Gardens Junior School

POKÉMON DESCRIPTION

Pikachu is a mouse,
Which lives in a little house.

Mankey is a monkey,
Who is very funky.

Bulbasaur is a seed,
Which has little reeds.

Magmar is a flaming duck
Which doesn't have a lot of luck.

Golem is a rock ball,
Which is not very tall.

Zapados is a bird,
Who can make a thunder herd.

Amy Natasha Whitworth (9)
Lincoln Gardens Junior School

WHAT IS GOLD?

Gold is the big bright sun
Gold is the tasty cream of a cherry bun
Gold is a pretty shiny butterfly
Flying in the sky
Gold is the tall daffodils
It's a shame that they die
Gold is the thin twirling leaves
Floating from the trees
Gold is the colour of bumble bees
Gold is the colour of the Easter bunny
Gold is the colour of lots of money.

Amy Hornsey (8)
Lincoln Gardens Junior School

I NEED FOOD!

Benjamin was riding along looking for food,
On his motorbike, he looked a dude.
He went past a newsagent's but it was shut,
He could hardly handle his rumbling gut!

Benjamin thought he was gonna die,
He could really do with an apple pie.
He turned on the music, he was gonna be sick,
When Celine Dion came on.

He was nearly out of the village,
When he saw a milk spillage,
So he went to help the people,
They were standing next to a church steeple.

Suddenly he saw a local shop,
It was selling half-price pop.
In the end he got sandwiches,
And he ate them like a hungry lion.

Nathan Wayne Fletcher (9)
Lincoln Gardens Junior School

MAGIC SEA

Deep in the water where the barrier lay,
I met children play.
A boy went diving so deep,
I went down a hundred feet,
Where all the mermaids lay
I found it was a wonderful day.

Hermione Cartwright (9)
Lincoln Gardens Junior School

THE MYSTERIOUS VILLAGE

Pauline was steadily riding past the local shop,
When she saw PC Fletcher their police cop.
She wanted some fresh factory food,
To take back for her son Dude.
Pauline entered into the shop,
She saw cans of Coke but no pop.

She heard a mighty roar,
It came from the attic door.
I'm sorry it's my lad,
He's awfully mad.
Would you like to meet him?
He's practising his greeting!
Meet my son, Guy Rilla,
He's quite a lady killer!

Louisa Vanessa Coombs (9)
Lincoln Gardens Junior School

WHAT IS YELLOW?

Yellow is the beautiful shining sun.
Yellow is the brilliant colour of a pencil crayon.
Yellow is the glossy colour of some apples.
Yellow is the lovely colour of some card.
Yellow is the bright colour of boxes.
Yellow is the gleaming colour of some paint.

Vanessa Justice (8)
Lincoln Gardens Junior School

What Is Blue?

Blue is the beautiful cool sea.
Blue is the lovely coloured sweatshirts.
Blue is the Scunthorpe football team shirts.
Blue is the colour of a new shiny car.
Blue is the glorious hot bath.
Blue is the small book.

Ashley McWhirter (8)
Lincoln Gardens Junior School

What Is Blue?

Blue is the beautiful wavy sea.
Blue is the bright cloudy sky.
Blue is the colour of our school jumpers.
Blue is the colour of a new shiny car.
Blue is a colour of a lovely splendid box.
Blue is the colour of a wonderful small bug.

Rebecca Escritt (8)
Lincoln Gardens Junior School

What Is Gold?

Gold is the beautiful car
Gold is the shiny colour
Gold is a wonderful splendid new car
Gold is like a lovely star
Gold is my glossy car.

Holly-Anne Rawson (8)
Lincoln Gardens Junior School

WHAT IS BLUE?

Blue is the beautiful never-ending sky.
Blue is the colour of our woolly soft school jumpers.
Blue is a shining and brilliant new car.
Blue is the amazing bright sea.
Blue is a lovely and colourful curtain.
Blue is a clever and helpful non fiction book.

Thomas Carnaby (8)
Lincoln Gardens Junior School

WHAT IS GOLD?

Gold is the beautiful shiny sun.
Gold is the lovely magical coin.
Gold is the furry bright coat of a lion.
Gold is the fantasy brilliant fire.
Gold is the colourful and lovely streetlights.
Gold is the splendid string toffee.

Ashley Godson (8)
Lincoln Gardens Junior School

WHAT IS BLUE?

Blue is the sea, the wavy splashing sea.
Blue is the colour of the summer day's light sky.
Blue is our beautiful snug school sweaters.
Blue is our car so shiny and bright.
Blue is my curtains so dark and colourful.
Blue is the bath water so sparkly and magical.

Gemma Rawlinson (8)
Lincoln Gardens Junior School

THE MAGIC BOX

I will put in the box
the silverest, shiniest star from the night's sky
and the fluffiest cloud from the day
the tallest mountain in the world.

I will put in the box
a whale that can sing
a cat that can tap dance
and an elephant that can do ballet.

I will put in the box
three wishes for the poor
the first step of a baby
and the last word of an ancient ancestor.

I will put in the box
a thirteenth month and a tree made of gold
a fish in the sky
and a bird in the sea.

My box is fashioned of the finest jewels
with the sun and the moon on the lid
with messages in every corner.

I shall change my box into a world of happiness
a world full of animals and trees
a world of no pollution, no traffic, no roads
I shall care for the animals which are in my box
That is what I'll do in my box.

Laura Cooke (11)
Normanby-By-Spital Primary School

SPOOKY WOOKY

Ghosts under floorboards,
Witches behind the door,
Spiders in their cobwebs,
Mice squeaking on the floor.

The broomsticks in the corner,
Next to a big fat rat,
The potion pot is brewing,
The black cats on the mat.

There's ghostly groaning noises,
Heard in the dark, dark night,
And misty images floating
Which fill me with fear and fright.

Bats are in the attic,
With big red scary eyes,
And there's skeletons sleeping,
Beneath the starry skies.

Yea 'Spooky Wooky' is haunted.
Why don't you come and stay?
I'll bet you any money
You'll leave the following day.

Christopher Williamson (10)
Normanby-By-Spital Primary School

MY TEACHER

My teacher is called Miss Gibbs
She wears these awful wigs
These glasses she wars
(Well they're worse than her flares)
They have really thick rims
And she uses them to look at her so called
Boyfriend Mr Symms.

Now the flares well for starters they are pink,
The same colour as the art room's sink.
She wears the most ridiculous earrings
All dangly and droopy.
But I must admit I do like her ones that are Snoopy.

She gives me these funny looks
Her favourite saying is 'Kids are snooks'
(Whatever that's supposed to mean).

She makes you work really hard
But never gives you a pressie or a card,
Tom's been told off by her twice
For in her desk he puts two fat mice.
She screamed so loud it brought such a crowd.

That's my teacher Miss Gibbs.

Rebekah Mayo (11)
Normanby-By-Spital Primary School

WE ARE RABBITS!
(Dedicated to my rabbit Molly)

We are not very tall,
in fact we are quite small,
we are furry and cute,
and we like to eat fruit,
because we are rabbits.

We love to eat carrot and straw,
and fill our bellies till we can't eat no more,
because we are rabbits.

We live in a hutch,
which we don't like very much,
we would rather be in the sun,
where we can play and run,
because we are rabbits.

We have a bed of hay,
which is changed every day,
so I think we will stay,
because we are rabbits.

Holly Darby (8)
Normanby-By-Spital Primary School

MY BEST MATE

Who's that ruffling up the mats,
Chasing all the mice and then cats.
Scatters the cushions on the floor,
And trips me up when I walk through the door.

Who's nosing into my pocket at night,
And comes out with his favourite delight.
Behind the chair for hours he sleeps,
Then crawls out for me to greet.

Who's all love and affection,
As he sits on my lap for protection.
He licks my hands and then my face,
Then off he goes for a game of chase.

Who's barking so loudly for me to see,
That there's a stranger at the door for me.
He is small and brown his name is Jake,
He is my best mate.

Katie Louise Bavin (11)
Normanby-By-Spital Primary School

PUPPY

I have a potty puppy
He's as crazy as can be.
He runs around the garden
And he chases after me.

When he's feeling tired
He curls up in a ball,
He needs a lot of sleep
Because he's really very small.

His favourite game is tug of war
He plays it all day long.
His great big ears go down flat
When he knows he's done some wrong.

When he's in the garden
He runs around a tree,
The thing that I like best of all
Is he belongs to me.

Samantha Reilly (9)
Normanby-By-Spital Primary School

THE DOG NEXT-DOOR

The dog next-door he's my best friend.
He wriggles from his nose to his tail end.
Bright eyes, sad eyes, ears pricked up.

The dog next-door he's my best friend.
Golden fluffy fur from end to end.
He barks to say hello but cats beware,
What's his favourite word' biscuits' of course.

The dog next-door he's my best friend
He rolls in the mud 'Ohh what a mess'
Off for a bath he doesn't think so.

The dog next-door he's my best friend
We lay on the floor, he's all snuggly and warm
But yuk what a wet nose.
His long bushy tail causes such a draught.

The dog next-door he's my best friend.
he loves his jam and toast but dribbles everywhere.
'Crunch, crunch' he goes where's it all gone?
But most of all he's my best friend.

Nichola Bratley (9)
Normanby-By-Spital Primary School

THERE'S A GHOST IN THE GIRLS' TOILET

There's a ghost in the girls' toilet,
Deep down in the sink.
It pops right out at lunch time,
And it's very, very pink.

Nathan Cook (8)
Normanby-By-Spital Primary School

THE MONSTER

There's a monster in the cupboard and it's a
Grumble grover,
Swift swurver.
Tummy rumble,
Mouth mumble.
Child eater,
Quick seater.
Bone thrower,
Tail tower.
Shy hider,
Drinks cider.
And it's staring right at me!

Amy Chandler (11)
Normanby-By-Spital Primary School

MY HAT

Here's my hat
It's silver and black
It warms my hair
It's round and fat

It keeps out the rain
It snuggles my brain
I love my hat it matches my Mack

There's me below it
And I love it.

Emma Cook (11)
Normanby-By-Spital Primary School

SCARY

What does Scary look like?

Well . . . scary,
and hairy,
and noisy,
and naughty and spooky and ugly,
That's what Scary looks like.

How does Scary move?

Well . . . he crawls,
and creeps,
he scrambles,
and straddles and rolls and ambles,
That's how Scary moves.

Where does Scary live?

In garden sheds,
under beds,
beside graveyards,
inside the bin, in pubs and behind wardrobes.
That's where Scary lives.

How does Scary eat?

Well . . . slurps,
and burps,
and gobbles,
and gulps and sips and swallows,
That's how Scary eats.

What does Scary eat?

Well . . . humans,
and mud,
and smelly socks,
and fish and chips
and stones and blood and chocolate,
That's what Scary eats.

What is Scary's favourite chocolate?

Kayleigh Crook (10)
Rochdale Road Junior School

THE SHOW

Let's groom and preen for the show,
And plait the tail of the horse,
We'll ride along with ample force.
Bounding along to vault the jump,
Clippity clop, bumpety bump.
Tally-ho - off we go.

We're at the start,
We'll stay nice and clean,
We won't be mean.
Hope the practice goes to use,
We've no excuse.
And now it's time to depart.

She's a chestnut mare,
She might be naughty,
Or she could be haughty.
She might rear up,
I could fall in the muck.
So I think I'd better *beware*.

Amy Downing (10)
Rochdale Road Junior School

THE SHARK

It lurks in dark places,
Under the ocean's surface,
Waiting for its prey like a dark hunter.
Its grey skin blends well with the dark blue ocean,
Like a lonesome shadow.
His teeth like sharp white daggers
Waiting to sink into the flesh of its paralysed prey.
He hunts at night looking for unfortunate victims
That might be lurking in his territory.
And when he hunts them down . . .
Snap!
Go his hungry jaws down into the meaty flesh
Of his unfortunate prey.
He does not hunt in shoals like other predators.
All he does is hunts alone in the dark ocean.

Jason Goodall (10)
Rochdale Road Junior School

IN MY BEDROOM

Laying in my bed at night,
On the ceiling what a sight.
In the corner curled up tight,
I think it's hiding from the light,
Looking like a piece of fluff.
All alone big and tough,
Silently it spins its web,
To make itself a silky bed,
And lay its tired spider head.

Georgina French (9)
Rochdale Road Junior School

WHICH WITCH

Which witch did it
And why did she do it?
Which witch did it?

Which witch did it
And who watched her do it?
Which witch did it?

Which witch did it
And what do you think she did?
Which witch did it?

Which witch did it?
We do not know which witch did it!
Which witch did it?

Rebecca Bradley (10)
Rochdale Road Junior School

MY MONSTER

M   y monster's mean
Y   ellow and green

M   y monster's stumpy
O   h he is grumpy
N   ose so big
S   ticky out wig
T   ongue so red
E   ars sticking out of his head
R   usty and dusty but I love him so much.

Sarah Store (9)
Rochdale Road Junior School

MY CAT

My cat is my friend,
Who cheers me up when I'm sad,
She brushes up against me,
And makes me glad,
Her eyes are shiny,
Just like glass,
She plays in the garden,
And rolls in the grass.

She purrs when she's hungry,
And growls when she's grumpy,
The best thing about Kitty,
Kitty my cat,
Is that we're always together,
And we like it like that.

Evette Brown (10)
Rochdale Road Junior School

MATHS

Mathematics how could it be,
one of the most important things for me,
long division and multiplication are the hardest of all,
they just drive me straight up the wall,
when it comes to tests I just go mad,
it's nasty, it's horrible, it's just plain bad,
the teachers they laugh and say you're dumb,
I'd just like to torture them,
'Mmm' that might be fun!

Tarnya Donald (10)
Rochdale Road Junior School

PLAYGROUNDS

Trees blow as slow as the grass moving,
Sticky toffee fingers,
People swapping Mars bars,
Papers blowing round and round,
Girls playing netball,
Leather footballs.

Children crying with grazed knees,
People shouting
'Goal, pass it to me!'
Playground as cold as ice,
Dustbins dark and green,
Year four's lining up for dinner,
So sticky toffee fingers and people swapping Mars bars.

Laura Skipworth (8)
Rochdale Road Junior School

THE STEELWORKS

The steel churning as it enters the boiling oil bubbling,
Spitting splatters on the rotten steel.

The oil gurgles with the laughter of revenge,
The shadows of the beast lurking in-between the pipes,
With petrol pouring out of them.

The terrorising iron flying all around.

The grubby workmen hammering
The rusting steel bars all day
In the cold wet rain.

Jonathan Wren (10)
Rochdale Road Junior School

MY FURBY

My Furby,
Is black and brown.
He's very small
With two brown eyes.
He's sometimes very hungry,
Sometimes he's not.
He loves to play
All day long
And sleeps at night,
Or in the dark.
My Furby
Snores like this
Zzoohhh, zzoohhh
When he's asleep
He dreams of a new adventure for the day.

Gemma Place (9)
Rochdale Road Junior School

PLAYING FOOTBALL

Children kicking
        People tripping
                Kids scoring
                        Drinks pouring
Children clapping
        Feet banging
                Children leaving
                        People cheering.

Paris Willey (8)
Rochdale Road Junior School

I WONDER

I'm riding in my spaceship,
For all the world to see
I've left the world behind
Now what's in front of me?

The moon flies by, the planets spin,
I'm speeding through the stars.
It's Mars I want to land on,
I wonder what happens on Mars?

At home I've got a rabbit,
I love to play with cars,
Does Mars have pets and highways?
I wonder what happens on Mars?

My favourite food is jelly,
And peanut butter in jars,
Do Martians have their favourite treats?
I wonder what happens on Mars?

Heidi Botfield (10)
Rochdale Road Junior School

MY FUNNY DESCRIPTION

I have a small nose,
I have big toes,
I have knobbly knees,
I have enlarged feet,
I have a red mouth,
Just like curtains in my house.

Elizabeth Snell (8)
Rochdale Road Junior School

A PERSON'S WORST NIGHTMARE

This thing lives down below,
Somewhere where you won't want to go,
He lives in a dark narrow cave,
Watch out for his friend, a skeleton called Dave.

This thing is a certain kind of guy,
A guy that likes to see people die,
He has teeth like razors,
And eyes with lasers.

This thing has a worst enemy,
He lives in a grave in a cemetery,
His name is Fred,
yet he has no head.

Craig Ryder (10)
Rochdale Road Junior School

THE TEACHER'S LOUNGE

What's inside the teacher's lounge?
Do they have a secret swimming pool?
Do they play with the toys we brought?
Do they watch the answers come up on a computer
                    and copy them all down?
Do they have weight lifters in there?
Do they have books of science to copy from?
Do they have acrobats there too?
Do they have TVs?
Do they cheat in the teacher's lounge?
What, oh what is in that secret place
                    the secret place is . . .
The teacher's lounge!

Leanne Brown (10)
Rochdale Road Junior School

DO I HAVE TO?

Do I have to go to school?
Do I have to do my homework?
Do I have to get a bath and wash myself?

Do I have to brush my hair?
Do I have to make my teeth shine, and make my face clean?
Do I have to eat my breakfast?

Do I have to wash the dishes with Fairy Liquid?
Do I have to do it all?
Do I have to wear these ugly looking shoes?

Do I have to make my tea all on my own?
Go to bed,
Do I have to?
Yes! Yes! Yes!

Danielle Brady (10)
Rochdale Road Junior School

MUDDY THE PIG

He rolls around in the mud all day,
He's really fat and he likes to play.
He is a really good lad,
He is never wrong or bad.
Everybody is his buddy
And he is the pig called Muddy.

Francesca Bradley (8)
Rochdale Road Junior School

ALIEN'S INVADING

You're sitting at home,
and a light shines in your face,
it's a UFO,
from outer space.

You try to run,
but there's nowhere to hide,
the light picks you up,
and takes you inside.

Now you're surrounded,
by little green men,
it will be light years,
before you see Earth again.

Leanne Sloane (9)
Rochdale Road Junior School

MY FAVOURITE SUBJECT

My favourite subject is games
when we are playing football
I think I am in another world
I dribble the ball across the pitch
and score a magnificent goal.

The crowds cheer happily
my team mates jump on me
I feel happy and proud
watch out Michael Owen
here I come.

Christopher Reed (10)
St Bernadette's RC School, Scunthorpe

Our School Sports Day

The lines are painted and the chairs are out,
The sun shines down, everyone's running about,
Parents gather as we take our seats,
The ice-cream van is here for treats.

Clitherow

We're off to the start in our sacks,
Jumping around like jumping jacks!
Steady hands for the egg and spoon,
Obstacles and skipping start very soon.

Webster

Mrs Sulkowski's at the start,
One, two, three off they dart,
Clitherow, Webster, Soubirous and More,
Mr McNicholas gives us the score.

Soubirous

The children shout, roar and cheer,
A runner falls dear oh dear,
They race to the finish we're finally done,
But the big question is who has won?

More

Adele Robinson (10)
St Bernadette's RC School, Scunthorpe

WHERE I'D LIKE TO BE

Over the moon and sea,
That's where I'd like to be,
The ripples of the sea,
Lots of joy and happiness under my tree,
That's where I'd like to be,
Or on an island where trees sway,
Making room for leaves another day.
That's where I'd like to be.
No guns, no wars, no fighting,
And where the sun is brightening,
The path to a wonderful day.
Where birds fly high in the sky,
On a cold winters morning.
And so at sea there to be,
A voyage ship to sail.
Over the rainbow,
Under the sky,
Let's hope the dream shall never die.

Lucy Coulbeck (10)
St Bernadette's RC School, Scunthorpe

MY WORLD

Imagine what it would be like with no killing.
No wars,
No fighting
No hate, just peace.
People would be happy.
People would think the world a better place.

Darius Zhabhi (10)
St Bernadette's RC School, Scunthorpe

A PERFECT WORLD

Imagine

Imagine a world where no one starved.

Imagine

Imagine a world full of peace and calm.

Imagine

Imagine a world with no guns and bombs.

Imagine

Imagine a world full of love and song.

Imagine

But just think of a world where no one died
and we were all together until the end of time.

Amy Gravel (10)
St Bernadette's RC School, Scunthorpe

UTOPIA

Imagine a world with no flowers, air or people.
I would not like it.

Instead

Think of world with no, rubbish or burglars.
Think of a world where no one dies.
I think I would like this world.

Natasha Trantali (10)
St Bernadette's RC School, Scunthorpe

IMAGINE

Imagine,
A world where the sun was blue,
Imagine,
A world where the sky was green,
Imagine,
A world where the sea was orange,
Imagine,
A world where the grass was yellow,
Imagine,
A world where the trees were purple,
Imagine,
A world where . . .

Naomi Powell (10)
St Bernadette's RC School, Scunthorpe

UTOPIA

Utopia is a place of joy.
We can orbit it from far, far, far away
And see houses made from sweets.
What a place Utopia is.

We can see people.
No one is poor.
Just imagine,
No war and no poor people.

So this is Utopia
A place called *Nowhere.*

Katie Trocko (10)
St Bernadette's RC School, Scunthorpe

BORING OLD SCHOOL

Cars and buses arrive at the gate
It's half-past eight,
good I'm not late.

Register done,
gone to maths
wish I was at the swimming baths.

Rush, push to the hall
wish it was break
I could get my ball.

Into literacy, out to lunch,
lunch box open
munch, munch, munch.

After lunch English comes, it's time to read our poems
after English, games starts,
then school parts.

Shaun A Mawdsley (10)
St Bernadette's RC School, Scunthorpe

SCHOOL

My mun said 'School is the best!'
I said 'I don't like the tests!'
My mum said 'I've just passed a test cleaning your room.
It was a right old mess.'
I said 'Oh! Mum I am sorry.'
Mum said 'Well, you ought to be,
because one of your darts, stabbed me in the knee!'

Shaun McDermott (10)
St Bernadette's RC School, Scunthorpe

IF I RULED THE WORLD

If I ruled the world, people would say please and thankyou and pardon.
If I ruled the world, I would make rules so no people would get hurt or
  injured.
There would be no more wars.
There would be no fear, just peace and happiness.
If all these wishes came true, my world would be a fantasy island.

Melissa Lo (10)
St Bernadette's RC School, Scunthorpe

UTOPIA

Imagine a world where people would play and not fight.
Think of a world where life was bright.
Imagine a world where people would talk and not shout.
Think of a world where everything was shared and not argued over.
Imagine a world where there was peace and not war.

Adam Brady Birkett (10)
St Bernadette's RC School, Scunthorpe

MY IMAGINARY WORLD

In my imaginary world *I would have a swimming pool.*
In my world, *no one would act like a fool*
and we would *definitely not* go to school.

Emma Blyth (11)
St Bernadette's RC School, Scunthorpe

A DEAD WORLD

Imagine a world without any oxygen.
Imagine a world without any trees.
Imagine a world without any people.
Imagine how empty it would be.

Katie Blackburn (10)
St Bernadette's RC School, Scunthorpe

IMAGINE THIS WORLD

Imagine a world that was always hot and sunny.
Imagine a world where money and sweets grew on trees.
Imagine a world that was perfect in every way.

Annabel Igoe (10)
St Bernadette's RC School, Scunthorpe

IT WAS SO QUIET

It was so quiet, I heard the snow fall,
from the dark dull sky.
It was so quiet, I heard a male ladybird
fly off a green soggy leaf.
It was so quiet that I saw a brown hairy squirrel
eating his nuts and it didn't see me.
It was so quiet, I heard an ant eating food.

Dominic Cummings (8)
St Michaels Primary School, Louth

IT WAS SO QUIET

It was so quiet that I heard the snowfall from the dark dull sky.
It was so quiet that I heard a male ladybird fly off a green soggy leaf.
It was so quiet that I heard a beetle rub its leg on a tree.
It was so quiet that I heard a big brown prickly hedgehog slide on the
slippery floor.
It was so quiet that I heard a duck skating on the ice.
It was so quiet that I heard an ice cube slide on the fat and thin floor.
It was so quiet that I heard a box slide on the icy floor with the ladybird.
It was so quiet that I heard a ladybird land on the moon.

Anni Blades (7)
St Michaels Primary School, Louth

IT WAS SO QUIET

It was so quiet that I heard the snowfall from the dark dull sky.
It was so quiet I heard a male ladybird flying off a green soggy leaf.
It was so quiet that I heard a brown hairy squirrel
eating some brown Brazil nuts.
It was so quiet that I heard a footballer kick the ball and score,
I was watching at home.
It was so quiet that I heard a cat purring.
It was so quiet that I heard Ann's hair grow.

Holly Brown (8)
St Michaels Primary School, Louth

I AM AFRAID OF . . .

I'm afraid of . . .
A wicked old witch that lives under the stairs.

I'm afraid of . . .
A wicked old ghost that lives in the haunted house.

I'm afraid of . . .
Big spiders because they are hairy.

I'm afraid of . . .
Vampires because they suck your blood.

I'm afraid of . . .
Mummies because they have paper wrapped round them.

Melissa Atkinson (8)
St Michaels Primary School, Louth

A COUNTING POEM

One octopus outside Oxford.
Two terrifying tarantulas tiptoeing to tea.
Three trees talking together.
Four frightening fish.
Five big flying frogs.
Six stupid snakes.
Seven silly Simpsons.
Eight elephants eating eggs.
Nine nosy neighbours.
Ten Thomas's talking.

James Borman (7)
St Michaels Primary School, Louth

I Am Afraid Of . . .

I am afraid of . . .
Zombies coming to get me.
I am afraid of . . .
A mummies' coming to get me
I am afraid of . . .
My sister when she pinches me
I am afraid of . . .
My brother's friend
I am afraid of . . .
Mr Marrit when he shouts at the boys
I am afraid of . . .
Gloomy ghosts when they come to my room
I am afraid of . . .
My brother because he shouts at me
I am afraid of . . .
My friend when we fight
I am afraid of . . .
Cats when they scratch.

Gemma Allison (8)
St Michaels Primary School, Louth

Five Special Objects

A hawk's head stuck to a wooden frame,
that stares at me
A gold dragon I treasure
A ring that I thought was magic
A shark's boney jaw.
An old compass that
gives me a headache.

Harvey Stott (7)
St Michaels Primary School, Louth

A COUNTING POEM

One octopus honoured at Oxford,
Two terrific tables tiptoeing to town,
Three thrushes thanking tanks,
Four fantastic fried fish,
Five fish frightened of fishes, *get it!*
Six singers sing song see,
Seven songbirds singing a song,
Eight eating eagerly eagles,
Nine nippy naughty newts,
Ten tenderly tickling tocks,
Eleven elephants eagerly engage,
Twelve tickling ticking tocks,
Thirteen thrushes are thirsty and throated,
Fourteen ferocious fighting frogs.

Charlotte Simpson (8)
St Michaels Primary School, Louth

A COUNTING POEM

One old otter opening the oats.
Two tiny tiptoeing tadpoles.
Three thieves who are thick.
Four fantastic famous frogs.
Five funky fish.
Six singing songbirds.
Seven snakes slithering.
Eight eagles eating.
Nine naughty neighbours.
Ten tenderly tiptoeing tortoises.

Luke Pocklington (8)
St Michaels Primary School, Louth

IT WAS SO QUIET

It was so quiet that I heard a centipede tiptoeing on the wet floor.
It was so quiet that I heard the sunlight burst on the soaking grass.
It was so quiet that I heard the frying pan sizzle
as I fried a wet soggy egg.
It was so quiet that I heard the wall shake
as I hammered in a screw nail.
It was so quiet that I heard the hair grow another
millimetre on the baby's soft head.
It was so quiet that I heard a fly rubbing its wings together.
It was so quiet that I heard the snowfall from the dark, dull sky.
It was so quiet that I heard a male ladybird fly off a green, soggy leaf.
It was so quiet that I heard an ant scuttle across the beach.
It was so quiet that I heard an worm slide across the wet cold floor.
It was so quiet that I heard a dry leaf grow.
It was so quiet that I heard an octopus tiptoeing across a river.
It was so quiet that I heard a snail sliding across the warm old rug.
It was so quiet that I heard Santa come down the red chimney.
It was so quiet that I heard Rudolph the red nosed reindeer
on my snowy roof.
It was so quiet that I heard myself grow.
It was so quiet that I heard a rocket land in space.
It was so quiet that I heard my pencil scratch
on my clean piece of paper.

Anne Hickson (7)
St Michaels Primary School, Louth

I AM AFRAID OF . . .

I am afraid of . . .
Aliens in trilogy because they have two tongues.

I am afraid of . . .
Giant octopuses because they have giant tentacles.

I am afraid of . . .
Jaws because it swallowed ten people in one gulp.

I am afraid of . . .
Big bears, which have sharp teeth.

I am afraid of . . .
Wild piranhas because they nibble on you.

I am afraid of . . .
Giant zombies because they bite you.

Matthew Evison (7)
St Michaels Primary School, Louth

I AM AFRAID OF . . .

I am afraid of . . .
Sharks because they have sharp teeth.
I am afraid of . . .
of vampires because they can kill.
I am afraid of . . .
Wasps because they can kill me.
I am afraid of . . .
An octopus because they hold you and drown you.
I am afraid of . . .
A monster because they are big.

Abbie McRae (8)
St Michaels Primary School, Louth

I AM AFRAID OF . . .

I am afraid of . . .
People with gas masks on when they come into my bedroom.

I am afraid of . . .
Zombies that come out of coffins.

I am afraid of . . .
Wars because they can kill me.

I am afraid of . . .
People dressed up in Hallowe'en costumes at my door.

I am afraid of . . .
Falling off cliffs.

James Hicks (7)
St Michaels Primary School, Louth

I'M AFRAID OF . . .

I'm afraid of . . .
Wasps because they sting me.
I'm afraid of . . .
Witches because they might turn me into a frog.
I'm afraid of . . .
The teacher when he shouts at me.
I'm afraid of . . .
My family when they make me jump.
I'm afraid of . . .
Ghosts because they scare me.

Rachel Dixon (8)
St Michaels Primary School, Louth

I AM AFRAID OF . . .

I am afraid of . . .
Mr Maritt shouting as loud as thunder.
I am afraid of . . .
Hell because he could take me down to prison.
I am afraid of . . .
A mummy coming to kill me.
I am afraid of . . . .
A witch putting spells on me.
I am afraid of . . .
A dark, gloomy, house with ghosts in.

Leon Murray (7)
St Michaels Primary School, Louth

I AM AFRAID OF . . .

I am afraid of . . .
Snakes that hang from the ceiling at night.
I am afraid of . . .
Rats because they have long slimy tails.
I am afraid of . . .
Sharks because they have sharp teeth.
I am afraid of . . .
Crocodiles because they have scaly skin.
I am afraid of . . .
A box of bombs because if they blow up they will kill me.

Chloe Hainesborough (8)
St Michaels Primary School, Louth

A COUNTING POEM

One old occupied octopus
Two tiny terrible turtles
Three thirsty trees.
Four fat fried fish.
Five flying frogs.
Six singing stars.
Seven swans swimming.
Eight eagles eating
Nine nippy naughty nits.
Ten tickling tiny tadpoles.
Eleven eager elephants.

James Leach (7)
St Michaels Primary School, Louth

A COUNTING POEM

One orange octopus.
Two terrific turtles, tiptoeing to town.
Three terrified, famous fish.
Four frosty, fiddling frogs.
Five feisty fish.
Six swimming salmon.
Seven sloppy slugs.
Eight electric eels.
Nine nasty, nipping newts.
Ten tappy, tippy toes.

Katy Van Kempen (8)
St Michaels Primary School, Louth

A COUNTING POEM

One odd octopus honoured at Oxford
Two terrific tigers tiptoeing to town
Three thrushes real thirsty
Four fat fish fingers sizzling in a pan
Five fish dive alive
Six snakes sing a song
Seven shivering stars
Eight eagles are light at night
Nine naughty newts
Ten hens in a den with Ben.

Christopher Lovely (8)
St Michaels Primary School, Louth

IT WAS SO QUIET

It was so quiet, that
I heard the snow fall gently
from the dark, dull sky.

It was so quiet, that
I heard a male ladybird fly off
a green soggy leaf.

It was so quiet, I heard a brown, hairy squirrel
eating its very hard nuts.

Darren Espin (7)
St Michaels Primary School, Louth

IT WAS SO QUIET

It was so quiet, that I heard the snow fall from the dark, dull sky.
It was so quiet, that I heard a small ladybird fly off a green, soggy leaf.
It was so quiet, that I heard a hedgehog rustling in the bush.
It was so quiet, that I heard a scorpion crawling across the landing floor.
It was so quiet, that I heard a comet in space landing on the planet Mars.
It was so quiet, that I heard myself writing.
It was so quiet, that I heard a bug ice-skating.
It was so quiet, that I heard myself thinking to myself.
It was so quiet, that I heard my heart beating.
It was so quiet, that I heard a group whispering in a quiet voice.
It was so quiet, that I heard the pan sizzling on the hot stove.
It was so quiet, that I heard another page turn.
It was so quiet, that I heard a mouse's voice.
It was so quiet, that I heard the chilling breeze from outside.
It was so quiet, that I heard a lunch box rustle in the lunch box trolley.
It was so quiet, that I heard a human being moving.

Thomas Richardson (7)
St Michaels Primary School, Louth

IT WAS SO QUIET

It was so quiet that, I heard the snow fall gently
from the dark dull sky.
It was so quiet, I heard a male ladybird
fly off a green soggy leaf.
It was so quiet that, I heard a brown owl.
It was so quiet, I heard a cat and a dog.

Megan Tero (7)
St Michaels Primary School, Louth

IT WAS SO QUIET

It was so quiet that I heard the snow fall gently from the dark, dull sky.
It was so quiet that I heard a ladybird fly off a green soggy leaf.
It was so quiet that I heard a black, hairy spider skuttle across the floor.
It was so quiet that I heard Santa Claus coming down the dark,
   dull chimney.
It was so quiet that I heard electricity, running in the thin wires.

Emma Hardy (7)
St Michaels Primary School, Louth

SCHOOL SUCKS!

School sucks!
Five days at school,
Is not very cool,
But it's a rule,
To go to school.

School sucks!

Six hours of work, work, work,
With disgusting Kirk,
Picking his toes
And putting pencils up his nose.

School sucks!

At half-past three all is over,
Have a chocolate bar called Clover.
Now it's the best bit,
In front of the TV and *sit*!

Jamie Freshwater (8)
St Peter's CE Primary School, Cleethorpes

OLD MR THORNTING

Spooky and haunting
describes old Mr Thornting.
He lives down the hall
and is very small.
He comes out at night
and gives you a fright.
He puts in his pocket
some dynamite.
So next time you see
Old Mr Thornting
Remember he is very haunting.

Joanna Barnard (10)
St Peter's CE Primary School, Cleethorpes

THE GADGET

The gadget is round,
it doesn't make a sound.

It is grey, as a dull day
and it likes to play.

The buttons are green
it has a TV screen.

He is very clever
I call him Trevor.

Ryan Spence (11)
St Peter's CE Primary School, Cleethorpes

MY MUM SAYS

My mum says I'm going down town with her but no . . .
I'm going down to the beach to get some candyfloss.
My mum says I'm going to the market but no . . .
I'm staying in bed.
My mum says 'I've got to go to my nanna's but no . . .
I'm off to my cousin's house.
My mum says I'm doing my homework but no . . .
I'm dreaming I'm in Africa.
My mum says I'm eating my tea but no . . .
I'm doing acrobatics at the gym with Emma and Lucy.
My mum says I'm at the beach but no . . .
I'm playing at Rachel's.
My mum says I'm in the bath but no . . .
I'm cleaning my bedroom.

Amy Waterman (10)
St Peter's CE Primary School, Cleethorpes

WINTER WEATHER

Winter weather's very cold
and all the colours are very bold.
Children play in sleet and snow
and then they all start to throw.
The snowballs through the air
but now the icy feelings near,
of Christmas Day with lots of joy.
Santa's sleigh is very near
the next Christmas Eve is in a year.

Christopher Mortlock (10)
St Peter's CE Primary School, Cleethorpes

THE DAY A CAT GOT STUCK UP OUR TREE

This morning a cat got stuck up our tree.
Dad said 'Right leave it to me.'
The tree was old, the tree was tall,
Mum said 'For goodness sake don't fall.'
'Fall' laughed Dad, 'a man like me'
'Easy this is, you wait and see.'
He got out his ladder and put it up against the tree.
'I'll have that cat in a minute, you'll see.'
The ladder slipped so he clung onto the tree.
Then the cat jumped down from the tree.
The cat was happy to be as safe as can be.
But poor old Dad's still stuck up the tree.

Lacey Burke (9)
St Peter's CE Primary School, Cleethorpes

A GHOST

A ghost, a ghost is what we fear most
Not this man.
This man was making some toast
When he thought he heard a ghost.
'Ghost, ghost wherever you are
Don't go away don't go far.'
'Ghost where are you?
It would be a pleasure to meet.'
'Ghost, please come out
Where are you?'
'Right behind you.'

David Curtis (10)
St Peter's CE Primary School, Cleethorpes

A POEM TO BE SPOKEN SILENTLY

It was so quiet that I heard a mouse scuttle across the room.
It was so quiet that I heard a raindrop slide down the window.
It was so quiet that I heard my pencil scratch across the page.
It was so quiet that I heard the storm coming.
It was so quiet that I heard the cars zoom down the road.
It was so quiet that I heard the heater humming.
It was so quiet that I heard the wind howling.

Chloe Chambers (9)
St Peter's CE Primary School, Cleethorpes

A POEM TO BE SPOKEN SILENTLY

It was so quiet that I heard a slug slither around.
It was so quiet that I heard the sound of a radiator.
It was so quiet that I heard a pin drop on a floor.
It was so quiet that I heard a leaf curl up.
It was so quiet that I heard an ant giving orders.
It was so quiet that I heard a rocket in space.

Nick Parker (9)
St Peter's CE Primary School, Cleethorpes

MY HAMSTER

I have a Russian hamster, that my aunty gave to me.
It always tries to bite other people when they come to tea.
In the night its exercise wheel squeaks and wakes me up.
I avoid to clean its cage out but in the end I just give in.
I don't know if it's a girl or a boy, although I don't really care.
Every time I see it he looks at me and stares.

Lianne Coultas (11)
St Peter's CE Primary School, Cleethorpes

You

You!
Your hair is like fur.
You!
Your tears are like shining stars.
You!
Your face is like a moon in the sky.
You!
Your nose is like the sun in the sky.
You!
Your mouth is like a crunchy apple.
You!
Your shoulders are like an orange ball.
You!
Your eyes are like balls of paint.

Chelsea Waterman (7)
St Peter's CE Primary School, Cleethorpes

Alliteration Number Poems

One orange hopped over the ocean.
Two terrible tigers.
Three thirsty foxes.
Four frightened rabbits.
Five fantastically famous frogs.
Six soapy socks.
Seven sweetly singing songbirds.
Eight enormous elephants.
Nine nasty numbers.
Ten tenderly tiptoeing tortoises.

Hafsa Begum (8)
St Peter's CE Primary School, Cleethorpes

YOU!

You!
Your hair is like a ball of wool all rolled up.
You!
Your eyes are like diamonds glinting.
You!
Your head is like a hollow tree.
You!
Your ears are like balls of fire.
You!
Your fingers are like snakes slithering round mine.
You!
Your legs are like sticks which are going to snap.

Claire Sleight (8)
St Peter's CE Primary School, Cleethorpes

THINGS I LIKE MOST

Going to cafes
Doing PE
Colouring
Going to the shops
Ice-cream
Art
Garlic chicken
Helping Dad
Going to the beach
Coming to school.

Matthew Brown (7)
St Peter's CE Primary School, Cleethorpes

You!

You!
Your head is like a football
You!
Your eyes are like diamonds
You!
Your ears are like pots
You!
Your nose is like a dark, steep hole
You!
Your mouth is like a football goal
You!
Your hands are like Dairylea
You!
Your belly is like a giant cookie
You!
Your legs are like tree trunks.

Jonah Simmons (9)
St Peter's CE Primary School, Cleethorpes

ALLITERATION NUMBER POEM

One orang-utan went over the ocean.
Two terrapins tiptoed to the tree.
Three thirsty foxes.
Four flying foals.
Five furry, fluffy Furbies.
Six soapy socks.
Seven singing songbirds
Eight annoying echoes
Nine pins shining
Ten little hens.

Sarah Stewart (8)
St Peter's CE Primary School, Cleethorpes

THIS LIZARD

This lizard it feeds on shoes.
This lizard it walks on two legs.
This lizard it wears a pop star's jacket.
This lizard it wears sunglasses.
This lizard has no cage, it goes mental each night.
This lizard drinks twenty beers every night.
This lizard smokes, he gives me nightmares.
This lizard can talk English, it is only five.
This lizard acts like it's a teenager.

Alex Crampton (8)
St Peter's CE Primary School, Cleethorpes

SHAPE POEM

In my poetry box there is . . .
A rough bead that I found in my sister's bedroom
A pebble that my mum gave to me when she left.
A furry ornament that I got from a package holiday
A glittery bracelet that my nanna got me from her wedding
A black and white feather I collected from a duck.

Gemma Sargent (9)
St Peter's CE Primary School, Cleethorpes

THIS CAR

This car blew up with the loudest bang I've ever heard
This car is the littlest car I've every seen
This car is like an ant's bus
This car is faster than a speeding bullet
This car is a remote control.

James Harrowing (8)
St Peter's CE Primary School, Cleethorpes

TEN THINGS FOUND IN A FAIRY'S POCKET

A golden tooth.
A shiny pound.
A golden feather.
A magic wand.
Some fairy dust.
A tiara.
A box of stars.
A small fairy dress.
A small picture.
A piece of rainbow.

Yasmin Spence (7)
St Peter's CE Primary School, Cleethorpes

I WISH

I wish I had a silver cat
I wish I had a golden bat
I wish I had a yellow pog
I wish I had a retriever dog
I wish I had a sparkling gem
I wish I had a really nice den
I wish I had an action man
I wish I had a dinosaur
I wish it could really roar
I wish I had a teddy bear
I wish I had love and care.

Jade Snowdon (8)
St Peter's CE Primary School, Cleethorpes

THIS MORNING . . .

This morning I got a kitten
I called it Jenny.

This morning my sister got a puppy
She called it Ben.

This morning my brother got a hamster
He called it Tom.

This morning we played with our pets.

This morning we fed them.

This morning my sister took her dog for a walk.

This morning we made our pets beds.

This morning we gave all our pets a bowl of water each.

Jessica Edwards (9)
St Peter's CE Primary School, Cleethorpes

I AM AFRAID OF . . .

I am afraid of spiders
I am afraid of gliders
I am afraid of snakes
I am afraid of lakes
I am afraid of a bee
I am afraid of a flea
I am afraid of bats
I am afraid of cats
I am afraid of pins
I am afraid of tins.

Jenna Young (9)
St Peter's CE Primary School, Cleethorpes

PEGASUS

Pegasus, Pegasus is a story I love,
Pegasus the winged horse that flies from above.
His wings are like clouds as white as the snow,
He gazes down on the people below.
He helped the heroes of Ancient Greece,
In myths and legends of which we speak.
A silver rain cloud in a clear blue sky,
Pegasus flew to help those near by.
The gods were so proud of what Pegasus had done,
That they gave him a place which was near to the sun.
You'll see him at night with the stars shining bright,
A great constellation of pure white light.

Eleanor Johnson (9)
St Peter's CE Primary School, Cleethorpes

THE HAUNTED HOUSE

The haunted house stands up high,
The ghost that lives there is going to cry,
You are doomed!
He's as fat as Mars,
Flat as a coin,
He haunts me at night,
He gives me a fright,
I can't see him in sight,
Although he haunts me,
We can see,
He's more scared than me.

Adam Brown (9)
St Peter's CE Primary School, Cleethorpes

THE UNDERWATER WORLD

The underwater world,
Is beautiful when it uncurls,
It's huge,
It's massive, so big I can't explain
It's aqua blue with fishes like a plane.

The underwater world,
Has great huge fishes like a snake but rounder and a lot fatter.
Some huge fishes have tentacles as big as a bus.

The huge underwater world
Has green and yellow fishes
Even curled up crabs in little red shells.

It is beautiful
The underwater world.

Gemma Kelly (10)
St Peter's CE Primary School, Cleethorpes

SUNSET

When I'm on the beach,
I watch the sun go down.
While the sea is flat as ice
And the sun is reflecting on the sea.
The sun looks like a squiggle of
Orange paint and a dab of red.
The sun looks like a beautiful picture.
When the sun is gone it goes all
Dark but when I'm on the beach
I watch the sun go down.

Betsy Fairweather (9)
St Peter's CE Primary School, Cleethorpes

THE ALPHABET

A is for apple which is very juicy.
B is for bananas which are yellow like paint.
C is for carrots which taste delicious.
D is for dates which are as black as a car.
E is for eggs that are white and orange.
F is for figs which look so beautiful.
G is for grapes that are juicier than ever.
H is for ham that comes in different colours.
I is for ice-cream which is cold as ice.
J is for jacket potatoes which are brown and white.
K is for kiwi that is an oval shape.
L is for lemon that is just like the sun.
M is for melon which is very huge.
N is for nuts that are very tiny.
O is for octopus which is very juicy.
P is for peanuts which are very salty.
Q is for Quavers which are a little bit curly.
R is for Roses when you get all different kinds.
S is for spaghetti that is very long and tasty.
T is for TimeOut which is chocolate Heaven to eat.
U is for under cooked meat which is horrible.
V is for Vito that is very chewy.
W is for a Wink Bar that tickles in your mouth.
X is for Xmas pudding which looks so nice.
Y is for yoghurt which is very tasty.
Z is for a zingy lemon pie.

Laura Smith (9)
St Peter's CE Primary School, Cleethorpes

THE MIXED UP MONSTER FROM MARS

The mixed up monster from Mars
Is brown and yellow from space
He lives in a junk yard
And eats all the rubbish
So nobody knows where it's gone.

His hair is where his bum should be
His nose is with his ear
His leg is where his arm should be
So he runs on an arm and a leg.

He never has to wear any clothes
So he just runs nude down the street
He doesn't know what a shoe is
So you won't want to meet his mum
She is as nude as the day she was born.

Adam Beasley (10)
Saltfleetby School

THE GOOEY MONSTER

Monster, monster everywhere
They can live in the bathtub
They live in the sink
They leave a gooey trail in your shower
Goo, goo everywhere.
They can slide under the door
And they can slide under the couch
They can live in the sea
They can live in your house too!
They can really frighten you!

Charmaine Gibson (9)
Saltfleetby School

MONSTER DISCOVERY

Green slime on the carpet,
Green slime on the bed,
Green slime down the corridor,
Green slime down the stairs.

Green slime on the door
And down the garden path.
Green slime down the main road
And through the public park.

I go into a cave,
Where it is very dark.
I hear a roar, I scream!
A monster's staring at me.

It was very frightening,
Terrifying actually.
A monster's staring at me
And I'm saying
'Please don't eat me!'

Jodie Stephenson (9)
Saltfleetby School

MONSTERS IN THE BATHROOM

They're slimy,
They're smelly,
They're disgustingly green,
Oh! And they're very mean.

Monsters in the bathroom,
Monsters in the sink
Monsters in the bathtub
And this is what I think!

They're sly,
They're clever,
They're having a good time,
The only problem is when it comes to bathtime.

Monsters in the bathroom,
Monsters in the sink,
Monsters in the bathtub
and that is what I think!

Martha Rees (10)
Saltfleetby School

MONSTERS AWARE

Monsters aware they are everywhere
Monster in the living room
It blows fire, it blows flames
It is totally insane and it's a real pain.
It zooms everywhere and it eats my teddy bears
It tears up the stairs and the living room chairs
And it doesn't care
It loves pears and it stares
It plays with my sister's hair
It likes riding white mares and
It hates people who sing.

It's green and scary
Not very friendly and scary
The thing on its tail glows like a crystal.
It runs like a tornado, eats play-dough!
When we made friends we said it wouldn't end
But he got hungry and swallowed me!

Jason Hill (9)
Saltfleetby School

Monsters, Monsters Everywhere

Monsters, monsters everywhere!
Creeping, crawling down my hair.
Monsters, monsters everywhere!
They are almost anywhere.
Monsters, monsters everywhere!
My mum says they are not there.
Monsters, monsters everywhere!
But I know that they are there.
Monsters, monsters everywhere!
Making noises on my stair.
Monsters, monsters everywhere!
Rolling, jumping, hopping around.
Monsters, monsters everywhere!
They are killing, so *beware*!

Abigail Geeson (8)
Saltfleetby School

It's Lurking

It's lurking in the school house
It's lurking near the sink
It's chasing the tiny school mouse
And now the mouse looks pink.

It's lurking in the cupboard, ready to attack
It's ready to eat you up now
So you'd better stand right back.

It scares me on my way to school
It flies over my house every day
When it flies past me I feel quite cool
My mum says, 'It's nothing, OK!'

Christopher Beasley (10)
Saltfleetby School

MONSTERS

I looked out my window and what did I see
A big green monster looking at me.
His teeth were sharp and very white
His scaly tail was out of sight.
He gave me such a fright
He had three eyes that were big and wide
His feet were as big as big as my house
His arms could almost touch the clouds
His breath was smelly, he had a big belly
With fire coming out of his mouth.
I shouted my mum and she said 'No - and stop being silly'
I saw that monster on that night,
He smiled at me and went out of sight.

Hayleigh Lee (8)
Saltfleetby School

MONSTERS

There are monsters everywhere
Monsters under the bed
So be careful what you do
Or the monsters will get you instead.

There are monsters in your bathroom
And in your sink too
So be careful what you say
Or the monsters will get you.

There are monsters in your living room
Hiding behind the chairs
So be careful where you sit
Or the monster will get you instead.

Charlotte Kaye (10)
Saltfleetby School

THE MONSTER WHO LIVES IN A HOLE

There once was a monster
Who lived in a hole,
He liked eating sausages
And big lumps of coal
And his face was all hairy
And he was very scary
And ate out of a very big bowl.
If you ever had seen a monster like this,
Please, oh please, give him a home
Because he's all alone.
He's all alone because
Nobody wants a monster in their home
Because he's mean!
Nobody liked him. Nobody cared.
Nobody likes monsters that kill teddy bears!

Laura Bishell (9)
Saltfleetby School

MONSTERS IN SPACE

He shot through space in a rocket
Saw a shooting star all of a sudden
It vanished and then you could see it landing on Mars.

A monster came out of the rocket
An ugly looking thing with spikes on its head and forty nine legs
With green and blue spots.

He had seven arms and three noses
Fifteen eyes and lots of hairs
About six hundred warts
Then he vanished and was never seen again.

Sophie Vines (10)
Saltfleetby School

MONSTERS EVERYWHERE

Drippy monsters under beds, solid ones in couches.
At night they come and eat all the crumbs.
When they wake up they come to eat your thumbs.
Sometimes they sleep, sometimes they come.
Sometimes they eat half of your gum.
If they come you'd better wake up or they will eat you.
They will hide in the cupboard
They will hide in your room
They will even hide under your shoes.
Before you sleep the monsters will stop you.
Monsters, monsters everywhere even in your underwear.
You must run, you must hide
Because the ugliest one has a bride.
Just don't go under the ground because
Drippy might be there.

Adam Mountain (9)
Saltfleetby School

METAL MONSTER

Beware! Beware! There's a monster in there!
Make sure you don't stare!
At night his metal goes cling! clang!
So make sure nothing goes smash!
So you want to know his name!
He's called Joe!
So remember - Beware!
There's a monster out there!

John Mawson (8)
Saltfleetby School

THE TERRIFYING MONSTER

Monster, monster horrible thing
Lives in your bathroom, lives in your sink.
He ate the fridge and destroyed the house
He terrified the mouse.
Just then we heard the car
So we ran down the road far
But we could not catch him.
He knocked into the gate and smashed our plate
He went tumbling out of the back door
Just then we heard a roar, so we fled indoors.
We jumped into our bed just then dad walked in.
It was really the one-eyed monster standing at my bed
I shouted 'Help Dad,' - gave a yelp
He left the house with the terrified mouse
That's all we saw of him.

Joanne Snelling (8)
Saltfleetby School

UGLY MONSTER

His fangs are sharp
His skin's got wrinkles
His body's got spots
He's as bad as a vampire
Drinking your blood in the night.
He is very hungry in the black sky
So you'd better keep away
Monster, monster in the night
As scary as a wolf in the moon sky
Now is in bed, time to beware
He might eat you, so you better be *scared*.

Wayne Bourne (9)
Saltfleetby School

MONSTERS

Monsters, monsters under your bed
There are some which have eight legs
Some are hairy
Some are not
But one thing for definite
They are very ugly.

Some have big round eyes
Some are tiny
Some are big
You may be scared of them
But really they are scared of you
I try to get them out of the house
Spiders everywhere.

Kerry Martin (9)
Saltfleetby School

FRIENDLY ALIEN

I gobble up sharp
jagged, yellow rocks,
from bubbling volcanoes!

I slurp red
hot steamy lava,
that dribbles down the
huge mountain!

I come from a ragged
red, rocky planet.
I forget the name,
But it doesn't really matter.

Emily Duncumb (9)
Scamblesby CE School

SEA

Look at the sea,
sparkling blue and cold,
deep as the bottom
of the world.

Listen to the sea,
roaring rough and wild,
crashing against
the rocks.

Touch the sea,
cold, gritty and smooth,
slipping through
my hands.

Taste the sea,
salty, spicy and mouth watering,
tingling on my lips
and stinging on my tongue.

Smell the sea,
salty, spicy and beautiful,
a wonderful smell.

Emma Benge (8)
Scamblesby CE School

SEA

Look at the sea,
sparkling blue, cold,
deep as the bottom
of the world.

Listen to the sea,
whistling, crashing,
wild as ever, smashing
against the rocks.

Touch the sea,
deep, strange,
hot or cold
and gentle.

Taste the sea,
salty, sandy,
not very nice
and cold.

Smell the sea,
seabirds feathers,
seaweed tangled in the rocks,
shells and stones scattered on
the beach.

Juliet Phillips (7)
Scamblesby CE School

SEA

Look at the sea,
sparkling, blue and cold,
deep as the bottom
of the world.

Listen to the sea,
roaring, rough and wild,
crashing against
the rocks.

Touch the sea,
smooth, warm and gentle,
swishing through
your hands.

Taste the sea,
salty, touching your tongue,
oozing down
your throat.

Smell the sea,
swirling round your nose,
rushing up your nostrils
like a sudden chill.

Andrew Lucas (7)
Scamblesby CE School

SEA

Look at the sea,
When you look at high
waves crashing against
the rocks and spraying
up into the air.

Listen to the sea,
crash against the rocks and
it makes a sizzling
sound and it makes bubbles.

Touch the sea,
it will make your hand
go all salty.

Taste the sea,
all salty and watery
and it will make
your throat all salty.

Smell the sea,
if you smell the sea
you will go all
salty and bubbly.

Jack Noon (7)
Scamblesby CE School

SEA THROUGH THE SENSES

Look at the sea,
sparkling godless and
blue in the sea.

Listen to the
sea roaring, rough
and wild, crashing
against the rocks.

Touch the sea,
feel the sea,
foamy and
splashy, tingly
on your hand.

Taste the sea,
salty and cold,
tickling on your
tongue.

Smell the sea,
foamy, tingly
up your nose.

Rory Hannam (7)
Scamblesby CE School

SEA

Look at the sea,
turquoise, sparkling and cold,
deep as the
bottom of space.

Listen to the sea,
roaring, rough and wild,
crashing against
the harbour.

Touch the sea,
cold, wet and murky,
slapping against
my hand.

Taste the sea,
salty, gritty and watery,
dripping on
my tongue.

Smell the sea,
sandy, moist and dirty,
blowing to
my nose.

Robyn Hopper (8)
Scamblesby CE School

ICE-CREAM

Ice
cream
whirly and
white and creamy
on a stand. Yum
Decorated
with a flake
stuck on top
and a crunchy
wafer cone
below the
white
delight
reach up
big lick
yummy
yum!
yum!

Harriet Hopper (10)
Scamblesby CE School

SEA

Look at the sea,
Sparkling, blue and cold,
Deep as the bottom of the world.

Listen to the sea,
Roaring, rough and wild,
Crashing against the rocks.

Touch the sea,
Splashing, waving and rocky,
Right over me.

Taste the sea,
Watery, salty and gritty,
Washing about in my mouth.

Smell the sea,
Sandy, hot and cool,
Flowing through my nose.

George Merrett (8)
Scamblesby CE School

INTO UNKNOWN SPACE

Into
a galaxy
speckled with
curious orbs, nine in
all. In front, the sun a
burning cannon ball smouldering
in the atmosphere. Behind, Mercury
covered in dingy, bottomless pits. Beside,
a sphere wrapped in a dense blanket of cloud.

Nearby, a globe quilted with blue, green and white. Next to
Earth, Mars, red with bubbling larva from a destructive volcano.
Beneath, a giant gas spheroid dotted with twirls of twisting air.

Above, Saturn a planet tied neatly with a lavish
yellow ribbon. Behind, a place protected by
its own sturdy stone soldiers. Around the
back of space lie two planets, isolated
and frozen, looking out on
to the unknown
universe!

Katie Lucas (11)
Scamblesby CE School

SEA

Look at the sea
Look at the sea
Sparkling, blue and cold,
Deep as the bottom of the world,
Listen to the sea.

Listen to the sea
Crashing on the rocks
And splashing in your face,
Touch the sea.

Touch the sea,
Feel all the salt,
And all on your hand,
Taste he sea.

Taste the sea,
Salty, runny and
Awful in your mouth.
Smell the sea,
Smell the sea,
Salty, flickering
In your nose.

Elliot Towl (7)
Scamblesby CE School

SEA

Look at the sea,
Sparkling, blue and cold,
Deep as the bottom
Of the world.

Listen to the sea,
Roaring, rough and wild,
Crashing against the rocks.

Touch the sea,
Cold, wet and splashy,
Feels slippery.

Taste the sea,
I like the taste of salty sea.

Smell the sea,
Salty, splashy and wavy,
I like the smell of he sea.

Emma Whitfield (6)
Scamblesby CE School

SEA

Shells on the sandy beach,
Eating fish and chips
As we walk along,
Salt and vinegar too!
Ice-cream for pudding,
Digging holes in the sand,
Everybody having fun.

Ian Askew (8)
Scamblesby CE School

SEA

Look at the sea,
Bubbly, blue and cold,
Deep as the bottom
Of the ocean.

Listen to the sea,
Roaring, rough and wild,
White as the top
       Of the clouds.

Touch the sea,
Sparkling, splashing and spraying,
Wet as the biggest
Raindrop.

Taste the sea,
Salty, cold and gentle,
Smooth as the finest
Glass.

Smell the sea,
Sandy, hot and cool,
Falling through
My nose.

Eloise Middleton (8)
Scamblesby CE School

SEA

Look at the sea,
sparkling, blue and cold,
deep as the bottom
of the world.

Listen to the sea,
slipping against
the harbour wall.

Touch the sea
feel the gentle water,
splashing against
your hand.

Taste the sea
as salty as ever
when I
taste the sea.

Smell the sea
lovely Mediterranean
slowly slipping
up your nose.

Jonjo Hanson (8)
Scamblesby CE School

A LITTLE SEA HORSE

The
Dainty
Dancer
Playfully prancing
Deep   in   the
Sea, his
Mouth a
Sucking
Tube. The
Bony body,
A   tropical
Creature. The
Bobbing   one.
Rapidly moving
His   single
Fin. It's the
Sea horse
With
His
W
A
V
I
  D   N
    N   G
     E

Hannah Priestley (9)
Scamblesby CE School

MY GUITAR

E   D7
A7   G7
E7   D
S
T
R
U
M
It strums one
Way and another.
It sounds high,
It sounds low,
It's as sweet as
A bow. It's got a
Body, it's got a
Fret. It's got a
Head, it's got
a Neck. My fat
Round guitar plays
'A' when I want 'C'
but it's a pal
to me!

Martin Lovesey (10)
Scamblesby CE School

COLD FOOT

Blue and very
blistered, it
shivers, excluded
from the warmth
of the bed.
Growing colder,
colder, getting
very close to
freezing point.
By morning
frozen!

C C C C C
O O O O O
L L L L L
D D D D D

Toby Hughes (11)
Scamblesby CE School

THE ALIEN PLANET

I lived on a milky planet
In the middle of space.
Bang! A bubbly volcano
Blew up my milky home.
Now, lonely, sad, bored,
I have nowhere to go.
Cold, gloomy, dark.
Space surrounds me with planets.

Jessica Noon (9)
Scamblesby CE School

THE TREE

The bushy oak tree
Sways in the wind.
Clinging to its terracotta
branches are the leaves.
Their veins turn off like
Rivers. Its roots like
Cement. Home to
hosts of
animals
cosy,
snug,
safe
and
secure
for
the
squirrel,
sparrow
and the
spider!

Eleanor Middleton (11)
Scamblesby CE School

SEA

Shells on the sandy beach,
Eating fish and chips
As we walk along,
Salt and vinegar too!
Ice-cream for pudding,
Digging holes in the sand,
Everybody having fun.

Mark Epton (8)
Scamblesby CE School

THE SPACESHIP

B-
last,
boom,
smash, clutter,
zoom, it's the
journey through
space, the universe,
the galaxy, all in
the Milky Way!
We've seen Earth,
Mars, Jupiter but
not Pluto. Now for
Lift off! Across the
dark silent Milky
Way! Through the
white soft clouds
We've
G O N E
too   far

Matthew Whitfield (8)
Scamblesby CE School

SPACE

Below the Earth, so tiny and round,
Behind asteroids *whizzing* through space.
Everything a black hole,
Comets flying by with a glowing *streak* of light,
Below me Jupiter and Mars,
Next to me an asteroid glowing constantly,
In front of me volcanoes *erupting* on Mars.

Adam Askew (10)
Scamblesby CE School

THE GOLDEN STAR

Still

glittering   The star
    twinkles,   it's   golden
shiny   at   night.
Brightly   it   glitters
in   the   dark, but   fades.
I   wish   I   was   up   with
the   star   so   smooth,
so   still. You   twist
and glide in the
twinkle   dark sky.   shiny

yellow
golden
star!

Emma Shaw (8)
Scamblesby CE School

WHAT AM I?

You cannot see me, I'm invisible!
I only move when you move.
I creep through cracks, under doors.
I feel cold or hot, but sometimes both.
You cannot hear me,
But you can hear my friend, the wind.

Answer: The wind.

Joseph Sears (9)
Scamblesby CE School

SEA

Look at the sea,
Sparkling, blue and cold,
Deep as the bottom of the world.

Listen to the sea,
Roaring, rough and wild,
Crashing against the rocks.

Touch the sea,
Smooth, gentle and warm,

Taste the sea,
Yukey and salty and water.

Smell the sea,
Lovely and nice.

Ciaran Melens (7)
Scamblesby CE School

MOUSE

Mouse scuffling,
Mouse sniffing,
Scampering across the land.
Mouse squeaking,
Mouse terrified,
Owl following behind.
Mouse hunting,
Mouse finding,
Looking in every hole.
Mouse tired,
Mouse exhausted,
Sleeping in its home.

Rebecca Downie (8)
Scotter Primary School

IN THE GARDEN

In the garden there are some bees
Buzzing near a few oak trees.
There are birds tweeting above me
Looking at my bunch of golden keys.
Fish in the pond swimming around,
Kind of dancing good and not making a sound.
Leaves are falling on the floor,
They are crunching up on the front door.
Butterflies are flying fast and firm,
Getting out of our term.
The grass is dying,
In the air it is flying.

Kirstie Howarth (9)
Western Primary School

THE SEA

Here is the sea, the wavy sea,
Here is the boat and here is me,
All the little fishes down below
Wriggle their tails and away they all go.

Under the sea, that deep blue sea,
Is lots of big fishes
And great octopuses,
Crabs and shells hurt your toes,
I bend down and saw a rose.

Laura Wheatley (9)
Western Primary School

IN THE GARDEN

In the garden, flowers grow,
When the wind comes it does blow.
In the garden children play,
They seem to have fun all day.
In the garden caterpillars crawl,
Because they are very small.
In the garden there is a cat
Who's chasing a very lovely rat.
In the garden there is a bike
And above it is a kite.
In the garden it is quiet
At least there is no riot.

Matthew Donner (9)
Western Primary School

THE MOON

On the moon
there was a spoon
floating in the air.
I did stare,
I picked it up for a quick look
and then I hid it in my book,
standing there far in space
far from home
without my comb.
It's driving me round the bend,
and I have no friend.

Adam Waterman (8)
Western Primary School

THE CLOCK

The clock struck one
My name is Don.
The clock struck two
My dad went 'Boo.'
The clock struck three
I saw a bee.
The clock struck four
Someone knocked on the door.
The clock struck five
I had a dive.
The clock struck six
I had some kicks.
The clock struck seven
I went to Heaven.
The clock struck eight
I had some bait.
The clock struck nine
I'm just so fine.
The clock struck ten
I made a den.

Christopher Turner (9)
Western Primary School

MAGIC FAIRY

Once I saw a magic fairy flying around my head,
At first I thought it was really scary, but no,
It was beautiful instead.

She looked at me and said, 'Give me your tooth,
and I'll give you bread.'
'If you give me it you will see that you can rely on me.'

Louise Blood (9)
Western Primary School

THE LITTLE SWEET

Round the corner in the street
I saw a little shiny sweet,
I saw something shining, round and fat
That twinkled like that,
I picked it up and trailed away and went to play.

Melissa Freeman (8)
Western Primary School

MY NEW SCHOOL

My new school is big and bright,
I hope to do my work all right,
The dinners are quite nice
and the tuck is a fair price.

Rebecca Smalley (9)
Western Primary School

IF I WERE AN OWL

If I were an owl,
I would soar through the air.
With my watchful eye, I would become a predator,
Swooping down on my prey, not letting them get away.
I would catch them with my claws,
And haul them across the floor.
I would fly back to my nest,
For a much-deserved rest.
After my tasty meal,
I would soar out again and fly up, up and away.

Lizanne Patrick (11)
Yarborough Primary School

IF I WERE

If I were a bird
I'd be a beautiful one
I'd be graceful and sweet
The innocent kind
I'd glide and swing and sing a tune
I'd visit places I've never been
Like Africa and America.
All the people below
Would probably look like ants
Scattering about the town
I'd whoosh up, up and away
Into the light blue sky.
At dawn I'd watch the glistening sun
Rise above the morning dew
I'd make a nest with twine and twigs
I'd go to the seaside to see
People having fun
I'd watch he sun set over the hills
While watching the tired peoples shadows disappear
I'd lay some special eggs
To hatch into my young
I'd watch the ripples of the sea shining
And see the other birds yearning
To be up in the air like me.

Hollie Meller (11)
Yarborough Primary School

IF I WERE . . .

If I were a swift
I would travel at lightning speed
Taking no time at all
Getting away from feline monsters
Before they can catch me
I would spot a tiny mouse
And a pink, juicy worm
Suddenly, the mouse would sense danger
And disappear in the tall, moist grass
But the worm would be easy prey
And would be in my magnificent beak
My shiny, yellow, smooth beak,
I would balance on my branch
Eating my pink strand of spaghetti
Looking like it was dipped in bolognaise
After my lunch I would take off
And travel at the speed of light
Around the huge world.

Richard Sharp (10)
Yarborough Primary School

IF I WERE . . .

If I were a star,
I would sparkle in the darkness,
Like glitter in the sky.

Looking down on everyone,
As they go out enjoying themselves,
And watching babies fast asleep,
Watching children getting tucked in bed.

I'd like to be the star sign Taurus, the bull
I'll have big long horns,
And a ring in my nose.

I could be a shooting star,
Or a star that stays still and looks down,
Seeing lots of adventurous places,
People having fun.

I'd be in the dark sky,
With the moon on top of me,
Up, up and away.

Catherine Wilson (10)
Yarborough Primary School

IF I WERE . . .

If I were a bird
I would be an owl,
A large barn owl,
Sleeping in the day,
While the sun is shining.

Then in the night, by the moonlight,
I would open my eyes,
Fly through the air,
With the wind blowing through my wings,
The night sky in front of me,
Looking down,
What's this, a little field mouse
Scurrying home,
As I fly down to scoop it up,
I will gather speed,
Finally, I catch it in my beak
And as I fly home in the night sky
I'll think to myself
Tomorrow again I will fly.

Katie Harris (10)
Yarborough Primary School

IF I WERE...

If I were a bird, I would be an eagle,
Gliding through the air, swiftly like a jet,
My beady eyes searching for prey down below,
I swoop down, fast as lightning,
My prey running helplessly from my sharp talons,
But I am much swifter and quicker.
I skilfully turn and fly up to the sky,
With a field mouse gripped in my claws.
Looking down upon the beautiful scene,
The air rustles my feathers,
High above me, the pure white clouds,
Down below me, the light green grass,
As I sour towards the clouds,
People down below as small as ants,
As I fly up, up and away!

Lucy O'Nions (11)
Yarborough Primary School

IF I WERE...

If I were a shooting star,
I would glide through the sky.
I'd burst open and brighten up the air,
Popping and cracking that's what people hear.
Looking at the landscape,
Trees and fields that's all I see.
Seeing all the brightness, people scream at me,
Like fireworks I swoosh and sway,
Into the clouds that's where I go.
Up, up and away!

Sarah Baines (11)
Yarborough Primary School

PLANE

If I were a plane
I would dash through the sky
Making patterns with my cloudy smoke
I would look down on the Earth
Watching people playing
My gigantic propellers like a blender
Looping in the air
The birds fly past me
Kestrels, swifts and seagulls
Down I go like a stone
That has been thrown off an edge
Coming to the land
The turbulence of the wheels
That have landed
Running down the runway
Like an ostrich running away from a hunter
Slower and slower and a *halt!*
And the brakes squeak
My dream is over.

Matthew Doyley (10)
Yarborough Primary School